RIVER HOUSE

||||||||||||||||||||||||||||||||||||||||||||||||

A MEMOIR

by Sarahlee Lawrence

Tin House Books

Portland, Oregon & New York, New York

Published by Tin House Books, Portland, Oregon, and New York, New York

Distributed to the trade by Publishers Group West, 1700 Fourth St., Berkeley, CA 94710, www.pgw.com

Library of Congress Cataloging-in-Publication Data

Lawrence, Sarahlee.
 River house : a memoir / Sarahlee Lawrence.—1st U.S. ed.
   p. cm.
 ISBN 978-0-9825691-3-9
 1. Lawrence, Sarahlee--Travel. 2. Rafting (Sports) 3. Adventure and adventurers—United States—Biography. I. Title.
 GV780.L39 2010
 797.1'21—dc22

                              2010007702

First U.S. edition 2010
Printed in Canada
Interior design by Diane Chonette
www.tinhouse.com

For my dad . . . with so much love and respect

I READ WALDEN ONCE

Marco and I crouched in a tent, sweating, while rain beat through the fabric. I held the napkin with the map on it. It was a cocktail napkin from a discotheque in downtown Cusco, Peru, meant to go under a rum and Coke. The sketch on the napkin depicted a two-hundred-mile section of the Tambopata River, which runs along the border between Peru and Bolivia. A single line squiggled out of some stick mountains. The single line became a ball of black scribble and had two words next to it: *los monstrous*, or "the monsters," the rapids in the inner gorge. The map did not explain how to run these. There were only two landmarks. At the top of the squiggle, two streams came in on either side of the ink river, indicating the beginning of the gorge. At the bottom of the scribble a stream came in on the left and there was a giant boulder drawn with a tiny tree on top of it, at which point we could trust the rapids would be done. From there, the single line ran off the bottom of the napkin. I looked at Marco, then out the door of the tent at a raging jungle river and wondered how in the hell we'd come to be here.

It had all begun with an innocent drink at that damn discotheque in Cusco. Marco, an Italian kayaker, was following the river seasons around the world. I, too, was following the seasons, as a raft guide and river advocate. Peru's water was running out, so Marco was headed north, and I was headed to Africa to run the Nile. We had been throwing back rum and Cokes with another guide, Leo, when Marco told me the Tambopata was running. I was curious about the jungle, tired of guiding tourists, and Marco needed someone to go with him, so I told him I'd do it. Heading to the jungle with a man I hardly knew was crazy, but he was dangling in front of me what I loved most: extremely remote, unknown water.

Leo was one of two guides who had been to this particular river. There were many reasons not to go. It was too far, too unpredictable, too hot, too wet; the place will ravage you. Leo had been, though he said he would never go back after the river marooned him in the even less-hospitable jungle. Amused by our persistence, he drew us the map on the cocktail napkin of the three-hundred-kilometer section of the river. With a drink for good luck, Marco and I were headed for a flooding jungle river, spiders, bees, and insane rain, with the napkin as our only direction. We left for the Tambopata at three in the afternoon the next day. Our journey would take us from the high, dry mountains of south-central Peru, down to Lake Titicaca, then between the knuckles of the Andes, just over the divide to where South America drains east.

Gunnysacks disguised our two craft (a cataraft and a kayak), our few worldly possessions, and food for roughly two weeks. We climbed on a lorry truck filled with crates, pipes, concrete, vegetables, and people for the forty-two-hour journey. The pavement lasted about ten minutes, then we endured the endless, potholed, bright orange road. Passing through the last little town of earthen buildings with days to go, I felt that the hours would surely kill us one by one. The truck climbed fifteen thousand feet over the Andes and descended into the cloud forest. I slept periodically on the uneven edges of the barrels, on the oars, the folded raft, and the kayak, but mostly I marveled at how my body shut down, resigned to the journey in that thrashing truck despite creaks and groans, despite cold, wind, and dust. I let my head fall over to look at Marco lying next to me, his icy blue eyes open but focused on nothing. Between the two of us, we'd seen a great deal of the world like this: cold, jostled, comfortless, raw. Often, I had been alone for such endeavors, and though even now my companion was silent, we shared the big white afternoon clouds and glacier-laden peaks tipping across our view until the sky went dark.

Two days later, with hardly a meal or a bathroom stop, the jungle enveloped us. Thick, lush forest rose at a low angle into the clouds, and the air lay thick on my skin. The truck dropped us on the bank of the Tambopata in the only town the river passes through, Putina Punco, a tiny, ramshackle village clutching the steep jungle slope.

We chucked our bags and boats onto the river cobble, moving quickly with the help of the other hitchhikers in the back. Everyone wanted the ride to be over, and some were going far deeper into the jungle from there. Within a few minutes, the truck labored up the rocky track and was gone. I teetered on stones out into the water and I stood ankle-deep in the fabled Tambopata River. Cool water ran over my dirty, sweaty feet, and I smiled at my journey, the past flowing to a single second of presence, everything beyond unknown.

I turned and started helping Marco unwrap our craft. I placed my two blue rubber pontoons parallel to each other on the rocks and grabbed the air pump. Once the boats were inflated, I strapped a metal frame between them and adjusted the seat. Sliding the oars through the locks, I sat in the middle of my cataraft, testing its blades. The whole craft was fourteen feet long and maneuvered from the middle. A mesh floor hung from the frame, and bags would be strapped to the crossbars. It was a small boat for the job, but easy for travel and remarkably stable.

A man with an official look to him, namely a green vest, showed up. "You need a permit," he said with authority.

"Who needs a permit for a river that no one runs?" Marco took over in Spanish while I leaned against my raft. The guy told us that one of us could go one hour upstream to a town where we could pay someone, and he would turn a blind eye—maybe. So Marco climbed on the back of a motorcycle with this "ranger." He looked back at me with that scruffy face and those bright blue eyes as they rode off. The river quickly flowed over the sound of the engine, and in that instant I felt suddenly anxious that I might not see Marco again.

By early afternoon I sat in my cataraft, fully rigged, still waiting for Marco. The Tambopata River rocked the pontoons of my raft while staring locals surrounded me—first hordes of children, then only men. The bank was littered with garbage, and I sat there for nearly four hours watching one person after another come down to defecate in the river. Women did their laundry, bathed their children, and dumped their trash. Flies buzzed around the discarded Coke bottles and cans of condensed milk.

Marco had told me to wait as long as I could, but if he didn't show up by late afternoon, he said, he would meet me on river-left, past the last footbridge a few miles downstream. We had agreed it would be best to camp out of town. The ranger told us the river route to this footbridge was an easy hour of flat water and riffles. Marco never showed, so as the sun disappeared over a jungle ridge, I strapped his kayak to my raft and went alone to wait where he'd told me to.

Breaking the cardinal rule of rafting (never go alone), I pushed off the shore and headed around the bend. Condors circled and landed on the rocks in the river before me. Plain brown birds opened their wings, exposing wild red and orange markings that looked like the eyes of a dragon. River otters played in front of my boat. The air was thick, sweet, and loud with life. *What a river*, I thought. This was exactly what I had left my Oregon desert home for.

The short, "easy" run to our meeting point turned out to be made up of steep, rocky rapids. I was caught totally off guard and my out-of-control boat wrapped on exposed rocks in the middle of the raging rapid. First, I sat in sheer panic on the high side of my raft, stuck and helpless. The river kicked up and grabbed at my legs. I looked to my left and then my right. Sheer jungle wall, green knots of vegetation clinging to rock cliffs. No road. No people. No ropes. I screamed out, and the river drowned my voice. My mind froze in sudden terror. No one should run alone, especially on an unknown river, no matter what anyone tells you. It went against everything I'd been taught—ever. The river spat in my face and mixed with my tears and snot. I got mad. Turning fear into determination, I stepped off the boat, planted myself on the slick rock my boat was wrapped around, and started heaving on the frame. I pushed and pulled and screamed and cried, slipping off the rock into the tumbling whitewater and pulling myself back up. I didn't even feel the water. I had a death grip on the boat, heaving it back and forth, trying to free it from the rock. Suddenly, the raft let loose. I jumped in and grabbed for the oars, but the river was too fast. I just spun around and wrapped on another rock. I wept and slapped the rubber tube of the raft, then climbed back out to push against the river again.

Hours later, drenched, I pushed to the shore where Marco was supposed to meet me. It was dark, but I could see the footbridge faintly against the night sky. I pulled the boat out of the water and tied it with two ropes to a tree whose trunk was a good fifteen feet in diameter and whose top I could not see. I hoped Marco would come to the water and meet me. My heart pounded with the sudden thought that I was still alone. Clambering up the shore, I scanned for shapes in the field. I called out, then stopped, reluctant to bring attention to myself, and stood there alone in the darkness, terrified.

Gathering myself, I wandered back to my raft. Hoisting my bag out, I slipped in the mud and fell into a mass of leaves and roots. My skin crawling from that touch in the dark, I swatted the leaves away from my face. I rinsed myself in the river and found a flat place in the field. Ravenous, I dug through the kitchen barrel for the stove and something to eat. I found my stove locked up by the humidity and bad gas. I shoved it back into the kitchen barrel and riffled through for anything to eat. I snatched a Snickers bar from where it had fallen between the potatoes. Peeling the wrapper off the candy bar, I took a giant bite and set up my tent. I climbed in and listened to the jungle scream at me. My muddy, sweaty arms and legs stuck to each other, so I didn't move in an effort to ignore the discomfort.

I was wide awake at midnight when I heard a motorcycle buzz up to the edge of the field and Marco's voice speaking with the ranger. Marco's feet dragged as he moved toward the tent.

"Why didn't you fix dinner?" he asked. "Where's my tent?"

"The stove doesn't work. Eat a Snickers. Your tent is on the raft," I responded flatly and rolled over.

The next morning, I woke up to the stink of decomposition and lay there for a moment listening to the rain. I pulled on a T-shirt and shorts, grabbed the napkin map, then climbed out of my tent and unzipped Marco's. He sat up, and I crouched inside next to him. "I don't want to run this river. We can still get back to Cusco from here," I said and handed Marco the napkin.

"No way, Shuggi. We're going to run this river," he said, shaking his head.

I rested my chest on my knees and looked at Marco. I wasn't sure yet if I trusted the guy. I hated the way men called me Shuggi, like "sugar" or "honey" or "babe." We had met three months ago on another river in a different town

11

and had run a few rivers together since. I knew him as well as any of the guys down there, but that didn't say much. I knew he'd rather be sleeping in my tent, but more importantly, I knew this expedition was more than I could fathom. I had always jumped into my life headlong—but I had an inkling that this was different. And I had fought my ego all night to be able to tell Marco I didn't want to run the river.

"You've got to trust me, Shuggi," he said, touching my shoulder. "I'll be there for you from here on out."

I thought about how the day before wouldn't have been nearly as terrifying if Marco had been there. And there was nothing as exhilarating as running into the unknown. I crumbled.

"Well, we need a new stove," I said. "The kerosene clogs mine."

"I'll go to town and get a new one." He unfolded himself and stepped out into the warm rain.

"Get a tarp, too. We can't be cooking in the tents."

Marco made the three-mile trek back to the village while I waited with the gear. Trapped in the white bubble of my tent, I felt the sweat drip down my eyelids and onto my copy of Henry David Thoreau's *Walden*. My mom had sent me the book when I left Oregon, right after my college graduation. I hadn't been much of a reader, but living in a foreign country for three months, with twelve more to go, made me crave my own language. So she sent *Walden*. I'm not sure if it was intentional on her part, but there in the dank, skyless snarl, that book filled me with a visceral longing for home.

For the previous four years, I'd been in one river canyon after another, and I'd finally hit some kind of claustrophobia. I was homesick for Oregon and for my family's farm. I wanted the sky that my dad worked against like a red ant, where we watched storms build for hours and flood east over the mountains before swinging north over the fields of fresh-cut hay. It was more than open land that I suddenly craved; I wanted to interact with more of nature's elements than just water. I wanted to get my hands in the earth. I also missed my father and felt remorseful that I'd left him to farm alone. I had always helped, because farming families pull together. But somewhere along the line I had developed the conviction that I needed to get out. I had abandoned my father and my family, and I wondered if I needed to go back.

I ignored these first stirrings of desire for a direction other than downstream. I rolled over in the tent and clutched *Walden*, letting Thoreau help me to accept going on as better than going back, despite the unknown, if only to "drive life into a corner and reduce it to its lowest terms." My mind went numb in the drone of drizzle on the tent fabric, and I ate one bite of bland bread at a time.

The next day, the river braided out around rocky islands, and I found clean lines through easy rapids. I was grateful to have Marco leading in his kayak. He looked down different channels and told me if they were clear and deep enough to run. Then, just as the jungle started to become comfortable, the Rio Colorado, a swollen red tributary on the right, slammed into the left bank of our chattery mountain stream and turned it into a massive red serpent. The river was thick with the crimson clay that is the base of the rainforest, and it was swollen to thirty times its previous size. It became one mighty current, river-wide. The helical flow ricocheting off the banks back to the center of the river obliterated the calm-water eddies that are a boater's refuge. My fourteen-foot raft felt like a pool toy against the amplified wave faces.

I swung out of control, hitting the outside of a right bend, when Marco saw the first break in what had become impervious jungle walls—a beach about the size of our two tents. He signaled too late for me to eddy out, and I missed the asylum. I slammed into the trees below, grabbing madly at their branches. Spiders bigger than my face darted through the limbs. Two of them fell onto my legs and were instantly washed off by the water that surged over the upstream tube of the cataraft. I did not let go.

For an hour, we worked to pull the raft back up through the current, trees, and spiders. The river whipped through dense brush and trees. Marco teetered down to me with a rope, careful not to become a noodle in the strainer. He tied on to the raft and braced so that I could let go of the tree and get onshore. We pulled together, searching for limbs to stand on beneath the muddy water. My feet slipped between cracks, and the current pulled me down repeatedly. We groped for branches and focused on the tiny beach until our feet were planted on solid ground.

The Tambopata flooded on a sunny day, no sight or smell or sound of rain as far as I could see. A sheet of rain came down at dark. Then it rained harder. I could feel the runoff from the forest gush under my tent. The beach felt like it was eroding beneath me, about to drop me into that gaping river. I stripped naked and darted out to dig a trench around the tents, which was cleaved into a two-foot-deep ditch by morning. It sounded like the ocean outside, eating away at our beach. I peered out the plastic window of my tent door into the dark and listened to the waves swat at the beach like big red claws. We were perched at the high-water mark with nowhere to go.

I had no reason to be certain that I would get out of the jungle. Ever. How was it that I was scared out of my gourd, but still driven downstream? I picked up my pen and scrawled in my journal: "I have abandoned the minute and taken flight. I left the simple pastoral life of a family ranch on the Oregon high desert because I sought the world. Surrounded now by the stuff of lore, I am flabbergasted at my inclination to go backward, against the trend of mankind."

I felt splayed as I watched mosquitoes bounce against the tent wall. I had been the kid who fell asleep on the atlas, picturing myself in the world beyond the confines of the valley I grew up in. And now Thoreau had me considering possible sites for a house. In that instant, with the river slapping against my tent, I knew exactly where my house needed to be—on the southern rise of the north forty acres of my family's ranch, the same distance from my parents' house as my parents' house was from my grandparents' house.

I'd never considered giving up my transient lifestyle, and I hadn't needed or wanted a "home." Was it just because the river had me cowed? I lay there, petrified by the water downstream. The forest wailed and closed around my tent. Some bug was eating holes in the netting. I clutched *Walden* and flipped through the pages. Thoreau had had a great deal of company in his house with squirrels and small birds. I didn't know what company I had, and if I should be grateful, or if I was right in my terror. Eventually I set the book down, because it had me questioning everything about who I was and where I was headed. Clearly I had enough problems in the moment without thinking beyond that river gorge.

The next morning, misty clouds hung low in the forest, contrasting the layers of dense green. The white trunks of the trees sketched across the horizon like pencil lines, marking the skeleton of the canopy. Condors circled down the russet river. Scarlet parrots as big as condors, with tails as long as their wingspans, descended upon a tree in a massive flock. The map on the napkin from the bar in Cusco, drawn over a week before, indicated landmarks of the canyon's beginning and end, but nothing about what was in between. Having survived the night, we broke camp. I adhered to the familiar and clung to the little things like stuffing my sleeping bag, breaking down my tent, and, especially, rigging my boat. The sediment in the thick water pulled through the net in the floor of my cataraft and slid along the big blue tubes with a constant low hiss.

We blew downstream all day to the last known camp above the canyon. The water was thick and hard to read. I couldn't see massive pour-overs amid the snarl of waves until I was on top of them. After a long day on the water, we found camp. Our map had marked a beach on the left above two tributaries coming in directly opposite each other. We found a tiny pause in the chaos of the bank and pulled in.

"Thank God we found this place. It's nearly dark," I said as I tied up my boat.

Marco just grabbed the machete and began to clear a spot big enough for our two tents. He was intent. It was late, and we were both tired and hungry. Then, as he swung hard at a bamboo cane, the machete's heavy blade ricocheted off and sliced into his shin. He dropped the knife, speechless, as blood welled slowly to the surface of the three-inch gash. He let himself down into the wet sand, and I elevated his leg over my knee. The moment widened into an endless green mass with us in the center like two tiny flecks, suddenly broken. Marco propped himself back on his elbows, head back, mouth open, no sound coming out. I pulled the cut gently apart with my thumb and forefinger. When I saw a flash of bone, I ripped off my shirt and held it tightly against the cut.

I took his hand and made him apply pressure with the shirt while I ran for a first aid kit. Except we really didn't have a first aid kit. I grabbed my toiletry kit and dumped it in the sand next to him—antibiotic ointment, a couple of finger Band-Aids, and duct tape. Nothing to bandage or clean the wound with. The only water we had was silty river water that we boiled for drinking. Blood was seeping through the shirt and dripping down Marco's fingers when I remembered the fifth of vodka I'd packed. I dug in the boat for the bottle and gave Marco a swig while I pulled his hand and my shirt away from his leg. The weight of his calf caused the cut to gape. I took the bottle and doused the wound with the liquor. Marco screamed and threw his head back as the bloody vodka streamed down his leg. I took another shirt from the dry bag and ripped it into strips. Pinching his cut together, I wrapped his leg with the cotton, then bound it with duct tape, ripping it off with my teeth. I used river water to clean the blood off his leg and hand, then went to set up his tent, leaving him groaning in the sand.

I laid out his sleeping bag and dry clothes. When I got back to him, the blood had drenched the cotton, but looked like it was slowing. I gave him several painkillers with another swig of vodka and helped him up. His face twisted as he yelled through his clenched teeth. Carrying the majority of his weight over my shoulder, I lugged him to the tent and let him down into it. I brushed the sand off his butt, hands, and feet and helped him lie back, elevating his leg on a bag. I rushed through all of this, quickly zipping his tent before the mosquitoes, bees, and sand flies swarmed in.

I stood there outside his tent, stunned, listening to him breathe. Then I walked out onto the rocks and watched upstream and down until dark. The river wasn't more than fifty yards wide there, but who knows how deep it was. With only a sliver of sky to judge from, I tried to predict the weather. The temperature had dropped a good thirty degrees. The rainforest was supposed to be hot and sticky, but I was bundled in my down jacket. Marco's accident made my thoughts and movements deliberate. The idea of losing him to some kind of infection frightened me. I was glad the wound was on his leg and not his arm—he could still kayak, and we could get out of there. Both of us on one boat was a death sentence. But right now, the water was too high and the wound too fresh. We would wait.

For three days, Marco and I ate pasta with salami, cheese, carrots, garlic, and onions. We drank coca tea with so much sugar we couldn't sleep. Home was on my mind the entire time. I wrote to my mom and dad, my grandma and aunt, but I didn't write about the river. I wrote about home. This would be a surprise to them when they finally received the letters, because I'd been talking about rivers forever, and nothing else. When I talked about rivers, it was in a language my family couldn't understand. My dad and I shared this habit, which drove my mother crazy. He talked about oceans and surfing, about the places he had been and the places he wanted to go. He wasn't your average hay farmer; he grew up on the California coast and was obsessed with the sea. We would talk back and forth over the dinner table about water. Not to each other, but back and forth.

"Dropping into waves triple overhead, and then that bottom turn at first light. The ocean made me strong. That's what I really need, to paddle every day," Dad would say, taking another bite of a homemade dinner. Things like that came out as non sequiturs.

Then it was my turn. "I've been doing sets of fifteen pull-ups to get ready for the spring runoff this year. I'm headed to a section of whitewater that could be flowing as high as sixty thousand cubic feet per second. The hydraulics will be massive, and rapids right on top of each other."

A big picture window framed the dinner table; outside of it, you could see a small garden backed by endless desert. Mom always sat so she could see the view. It was the view she liked best in the world. It was her life's work. She wasn't much of a swimmer, even in flat water, and hated to get her head wet. She let us volley back and forth about the other worlds we dreamed of. Never much talk about the ranch or the desert or what we loved about it or what we wanted to do there. We lived there and kept the horses and cattle and dogs and chickens and cats alive, but our minds had wandered off years ago, and they rarely returned. In any case, I wrote about the ranch there in that soggy jungle, inspired by a river that would just as soon drown me.

When Marco's bandages started to stink, I boiled them and redressed his wound twice a day to fight infection. We talked about rivers. The big ones: the Zambezi, the Futa, the Slave. We reassured ourselves that we'd seen bigger water. The thing we left unsaid was that some rivers carry their water better than others. If large-volume rivers are voluptuous, then the Tambopata was morbidly obese. We held our ground on the thin gray line between the river and the jungle. One night I lay in my tent, naked on top of my sleeping bag. I couldn't sleep. "Marco?" I whispered through the walls of our tents.

"What, Shuggi?"

"I want to go home."

"Just make home wherever you go."

I rolled over and thought of the old Masai man who said to me once, "Melakua ang inchu"—*You're never far from home as long as you're alive.* He taught me that home is in the heart and mind's eye. Home is a place, but it is also the strength you take on your peregrinations. It is roots grounded in place; it is wings governed by no place. His father had taught him this when he was young, becoming a lion hunter. Home is never far *as long as you're alive.*

By five on the third morning, I sat clutching our napkin with the map on it. That black squiggle of rapids had my attention. The water hadn't dropped at all. In fact, the river had been on the rise the whole time. I couldn't sleep through the thunder of massive boulders shifting in the riverbed. The rain hadn't stopped while we waited, and it did not look like it would break anytime soon. The food that we'd bought two weeks before in Cusco was dwindling. Heading downstream was the only way out. Marco and I decided to go. The understanding that we had only one option terrified me, but also let me step forward with confidence. That, too, was the only option.

I unwrapped Marco's bandage, and my gut turned at the sight of the yellow, puffed edges of the wound. Still, it was knitting up despite the tropics and the mud. I boiled his bandage again and put it back on wet. It would get wet anyway. He packed his bag and tent while I rigged to flip, pulling the cam straps extra tight, ready for anything. I dragged Marco's kayak down to the river and helped him in. I tried to remember everything I had ever learned or been told about whitewater, chiefly never to let go of the boat, even if I flipped.

As I climbed into the raft, a tree slammed into the side of my boat, its roots raw and wild, slapping my face. On many rivers you can see driftwood and other deposits high in the trees. We were already high in the trees, and I saw no indication that the river had ever run higher. The water wasn't held by the banks anymore; it was held by the mountains.

The light was flat, and the forest hung over continuous rapids. A dogged current and walloping waves funneled into a mess of holes and hydraulics the size of buildings. The holes and falls swallowed half the river in places. Out of options, I read the river and ran without hesitation. My life depended on my ability to turn fear into focus. My mind and body had to be quicker than the river.

There were no lines in the rapids. The river sucked my boat into holes and held me there, spinning the raft before spitting me out. I bent my oar and heard the metal frame flex and crack. River waves are usually consistent, but these waves behaved like a stormy sea. Surges lifted me off my path into the meat of the whitewater I was trying to skirt. It was a monster of a river, but easier to negotiate with than the jungle banks. And in between the terror and the waves was true pleasure. Dancing with the river was my passion. In the midst of something so massive and out of my control, I could find peace. Peace like nowhere else.

Our precious napkin showed the landmarks that would indicate the end of the gorge and the beginning of the flats, a boulder the size of a two-story American house and a tributary entering there on river-left. As the river screamed around a left bend, I saw it. Our landmark rock stuck out about three feet. It was the first rock we'd seen since the Rio Colorado, and on any other day I might have missed it. I couldn't believe a rock the size of a two-story house was almost completely buried beneath the water.

The tributary on river-left had blown its banks. I blasted up on the pillow of water piled on the upstream side of the boulder and slid off it to the right. A short while later, the river calmed and flattened out like a fat snake in the sun. I tucked my oars under my knees and looked up for the first time. Marco started to play in his kayak. We talked a little and watched for birds. The canyon was done.

Our camp that night was the flattest one we'd found. I briefly explored the woodland barricade, but found it positively impenetrable. I imagined root balls and bugs overtaking me, leaving nothing but my sunglasses and my copy of *Walden* sitting there open to a page with a single underlined passage: "I went to the woods because I wished to live deliberately, to front only the essential facts of life, and see if I could learn what it had to teach." All I wanted was to survive what the jungle had to teach, so I could get back to a place I could comprehend.

More and more, I wanted the desert. When Marco asked me why on earth I had left the sky-dominated lands of my home, I didn't have an answer, but I thought about it. Maybe I just needed the jungle to realize I had a home. For the first time, I wanted to go back. I was ready to explore my own place for once, to live and work each season in an ecosystem as familiar as Sunday breakfast. I stared out at the river, but it wasn't taking me home. Not yet. I had another ten months planned. First back to Cusco, then to Africa to run a thousand miles of the Blue Nile, then Costa Rica, Colombia, Peru again, Argentina, Chile—rivers, rivers, rivers. Guiding, training, expeditions, advocacy. My new realizations seemed irrelevant.

The fog burned off the next morning, leaving the jungle a vibrant new place. We dried our tents and wet clothes for the first time in eleven days. I scrubbed Marco's leg with a scarf over my nose, agitated pus dribbling down his calf. I dressed the wound with a fresh shirt, and we pushed downstream onto the glassy water of the plains, down a river with so little gradient that in most places there was no perceptible current. A jaguar stood almost invisible against the texture of the river stones. A two-meter caiman slid off the bank while monkeys with tan faces played in the trees. Somewhere in the fat part of South America, headed to the Atlantic, I tried to grasp the incomprehensible nature of the Amazon watershed. It was just a matter of endurance at that point. We had another five days of flat water. Marco and I continued to find things to talk about, although there was a lot of comfortable silence. His cut was healing, and I wasn't worried about him losing his leg anymore, but he still needed the hospital in Cusco. The jungle seemed bigger and more beautifully complex than it had before, as I watched at least two dozen different kinds of butterflies land on my boat, every shade of yellow, orange, and red, neon green and iridescent blue.

I helped Marco get up on the raft with his kayak at lunchtime. We floated downstream. I straddled the back tube as if it were a big blue banana and finished reading *Walden*. Dangling my feet in the water, I allowed the current to play with them where deep rocks disturbed the almost perfect layers of laminar flow. Between chapters, I wiggled my toes and watched the jungle slide by. I wondered when all these rivers would flow toward home instead of endlessly into each other.

For four more days, we erected our placeless home on sandy rises and gravel bars. The jungle sounded like a war zone, with frogs that went off like machine guns on rapid fire. The moon rose and lit up my tent as I tried to fall asleep. On the fifth morning, we woke at first light with the birds. There was nothing lyrical about anything that lived in the rainforest, and if that place was awake, so were we. We waited for our tents to dry, because dew in the jungle was like a hard rain in the desert. When we left it was hot and still, and I pushed for only two hours before we came to the Tambopata Research Center and a whole string of motorboats. The people here were the first we'd seen in weeks. Even though motors were prohibited on most of the Tambopata River, we thought we heard the faint buzz of an engine over breakfast. But we dismissed it; we had heard a lot of things in the forest. And the jungle seemed like it would never end.

As we pulled up, a cargo boat was getting ready to launch, and they agreed to give us a ride to the confluence of the Rio

Madre de Dios and the town there. We de-rigged in ten minutes. The cataraft tubes were still deflating as the boat pulled away from the dock. The jungle went by like a film. What would have taken us another six days took only six hours in the boat, a dugout from a tree that must have measured eight feet in diameter. Our captain wore only cutoff jeans and aviator sunglasses. He held a beautiful woman on his lap, her long black hair flowing past the left side of his face.

This marked the beginning of many more days of travel to get back out of the jungle. Dugout to motorcycle taxi to four-by-four truck to bus with six-foot jungle tires to rickety local bus with normal-size tires: Cusco was even farther than before. I leaned against the rough-sawn innards of the dugout, throwing my arm over the edge into the wake spray, and let a final sense of relief sink in. Each river I ran became more challenging. Each time, my escape narrowed. As we banked around a bend in the river, the sun hit my face, and I thought back to the single rapid that had set me on this course.

FIRST KISS

At river mile 179 in the Grand Canyon, the Colorado River comes to a brink and drops away over a rapid that's distinct from any other. A million years ago, the Colorado was dammed there by a lava flow. For a thousand years the Grand Canyon held a giant reservoir. I imagine the lava dam breaking away in a writhing mass of water, whipping suddenly from stagnant green to frothing brown. It bursts and kicks and spits and looks totally unrunnable. The rapid is massive and deafening. Today we call it Lava Falls.

When I first rowed it, three years before my Tambopata run, I was just a sophomore in college and had never rowed a gear raft before in my life. I had a little experience with rafts and an Australian river guide boyfriend who got me the coveted chance to run the Colorado River in the spring. So I took a month off from school and flew to Arizona.

For two weeks, I fought the river as it swatted my boat and knocked me sideways. I strained against the oars, trying to hold my line. Every rapid felt like a chaotic pummeling. It was a flat-water day until the afternoon when we would run Lava Falls. I tucked my oars under my knees and looked down at my blistered hands. I rubbed them lightly on my thighs and looked up. The canyon rim was out of sight; a cliff face was all I could see. I felt my heart beating against my chest and anxiety lurching in my stomach. I took a deep breath and held it in, then listened to my own pulse.

The guide floating beside me in a wooden dory had on a pair of fresh shorts that he'd saved for thirteen days as a sort of offering. The upstream wind felt like a hair dryer, chapping my lips. I lowered my head, closed my eyes, then reopened them to look at the emerald green water in front of my yellow raft. Coming around the last bend, I was looking out at my oar when the other guides signaled to pull over.

I tied up my boat for the scout, but didn't take my life jacket off. Instead, I cinched it down, my sandals too, and started up the trail between basalt boulders. When I got to the scouting rock where the other guides had gathered, I stood back and looked at the falls for the first time. The canyon walls laid shadows across the whitewater and took the glare off it.

I listened to the senior guides as they talked about how to run the river. Enter on the bubble line because you won't be able to see the rapid from above it. Run right. Hit the V-wave straight. If you don't flip there, line up for the mountain waves at the bottom. That was the gist of it—enough information for me. It wasn't as if I'd have control of my boat anyway. I left them there, talking and pointing. I looked back a couple of times on my way to my raft, double-checking my entry, walking a trail well worn from thousands of boaters previewing their fate.

I pushed off the sharp black basalt with my right foot, drifting out into the eddy after I pulled out my sand stake. Both my feet met on the fat yellow tube of my boat. I maneuvered around the firewood, dry bags, and cooler to my seat in the middle, where I took hold of the oars. Their black rubber handles felt solid in my grip. The blades, more than ten feet away, were an extension of myself as I slipped them into the water. The calm but consistent backwater current pulled on my arm. Contact.

The other guides moved back to their boats and got ready to run. They each made eye contact and gave a nod before we pulled out in a lineup. I pulled in last, watching each boat drop out of sight. As I approached the brink, the sound hit me, and the boat in front of me flipped. I put my right tube on the bubble line and dropped in.

In that instant, the world slowed down. Silence and the deliberate placement of my oars into the comforting resistance of current was something I had never felt before. My ten-foot arms did not flail and dive; they were steady. I scanned waves and holes, totally oriented. I caught the corner of the ledge hole and it sent me straight into the V-wave. Leaning forward, I braced my oars so the crashing waves on either side of me couldn't knock them out of my hands. I didn't feel the water that blasted my body and buried the raft. In that instant, under all that water, the river pulled me close, whispered in my ear, and showed me something wild.

Whatever I was, I was minuscule next to the two massive, choking holes on either side of me. Totally submerged in the aerated white, I reappeared on the face of a breaking wave. It felt like it took years to get to the top. I shot over the lip and leaned back as the boat dropped vertically into the trough, then back up again. A breaking wave blocked my boat, wrapped its strong, wet fingers around me, and squeezed. For a moment, I didn't matter. Nothing mattered. On the other side of the wave my eyes were open and my hands were on the oars. Disoriented from being right side up instead of upside down, I sidled slightly to the left and lined up for the mountains. Time dilated. I took a breath, waited, then stood and leaned on the oars. The boat climbed the first wave for what seemed like forever. I wondered if the bow would tip beyond 90 degrees and topple over backward. My oars were planted like the submerged fins of a ship to keep it from rolling in rough seas. The bow blasted through the lip of the wave, drenching me. Water streamed under my clothes. Pitching down the backside, my body shuddered. When I blew out the bottom of the rapid into the flat water, I leaned back, my oars under my knees, twirling on downstream. There was a sense of mercy and ease as I released the grip on the black rubber handles, my hands cramped and white. That day, the river took a dusty desert girl and made her an insatiable river runner. It was the beginning of my endless search for those dilated moments in the midst of something massive and wild.

The following summer, at the age of nineteen, I was guiding rafts on rivers all over the Sierra foothills, on my way from the

Tuolumne River outside Yosemite National Park, north to the American River. I was single, wearing a bikini top and a pair of shorts. The air-conditioning in my car wasn't working, so I had my window down, my left foot dangling out of it. My back was sticking to the seat. I pulled into Groveland, California, in time to meet a friend for a drink. The bar was in the oldest building in town and stood stately on the south side of the road. I parked, threw on a T-shirt, and didn't bother rolling up the windows.

I found my friend, John, sitting at the bar, hovering over some whiskey. It looked like a swill joint for cowboys and wild women. I smiled at the old pictures of the Hetch Hetchy Valley before the dam went in as I sat on the stool next to my friend. He gave me a hug and ordered me a whiskey.

"So, you're guiding."

"Yeah, trying," I said and sipped my drink.

"I've got a river for you."

"Oh yeah?"

He smiled and blinked slowly. "Yeah. It's called the Futaleufú. The whitewater is huge." He finished his whiskey and asked for another. "The water is aqua blue and so clear, you can see people getting tossed around twenty feet under when they fall out of your boat."

My laugh got giddy. "Where is it?"

Chilean Patagonia. And they want to dam it." His dark hair was shaggy, and the tops of his hands brown. He wore a threadbare Western shirt to keep the sun off. He mentioned the dam like it was no surprise. A few people like to run rivers, but a lot more people like dependable, renewable power. My gut turned at the thought of it.

John glanced at me. "Want another drink?" he asked.

"No, thanks," I said. "I have to drive." My next river trip was a hundred miles away and I had to rig at seven o'clock the next morning. I left him at the bar and headed downstream.

After that mention, I never could let go of the Futaleufú River. All I could think about was that river with the aqua blue water. My heart quickened, and the river's pulse trumped my own. I had to see it. My life narrowed like the sight of a gun on that river. I applied for a Thomas J. Watson Fellowship, which funds graduating seniors to travel outside the United States for one year to pursue their passion, typically nonacademic. My passion was the Futaleufú, and that obsession was at the heart of my proposal when I put my dream year on paper. I proposed a journey to explore rivers. Big rivers. Not just the Futaleufú, but rivers the color of mud, bottomless emerald green, glacial blue, and clear turquoise. Rivers that drain entire continents and writhe like serpents at the bottom of steep gorges. Myths and legends were all that I knew of the canyons and water that would dictate that year of my life. I expected holes the size of buildings and miles of continuous Class V rapids. I wanted to explore the stories of people and time, and the smoothing of rocks. It was more than a lustful affair with whitewater; I had gotten it into my mind at some point while hauling hay or driving tractors on the family ranch in Oregon that I wanted to spend my life conserving, restoring, and cleaning the arteries of the planet.

There is something about a dream that is supposed to stay in another consciousness and not mingle with reality. Not long after receiving the fellowship and directly after graduation, I would fly to Peru for three months, then travel to East

Africa for three months, then return to Costa Rica, Colombia, and Peru. I would make my way to Chile by Christmas and spend the remainder of the year on the Futaleufú. I had a few contacts and trips lined up, but mostly I would let the year take its own shape. Shortly after the overwhelming excitement of receiving the fellowship subsided, I realized that I would in fact have to complete a proposal that it scared me just to read, and I started to pull my eyelashes out. I had nightmares about getting ravaged by crocodiles and rivers flowing uphill. I swam laps in the college swimming pool repeatedly in a single breath, because I thought drowning could be a distinct possibility in my near future.

HEARTHSTONE

Three months into my Watson year, I was getting what I bargained for and maybe more. Five days after the motorboat picked me and Marco up, the jungle seemed worlds away. I stepped back into my apartment in the upper San Blas hills of Cusco, Peru. Before our trip, I had been camped out there for two months while working as a river guide on the Apurimac River. At twelve thousand feet, the temperature hovered in the midforties. The room was bare, with mauve walls and a linoleum floor. I was back for a few weeks of guiding before heading to Africa, so I settled in, spreading my sleeping bag on a thin pad in one corner and hanging my rafting gear on the wall. A piece of duct tape fixed a photo of my parents next to my bed, about one foot off the floor. I lay there studying their faces. In the photo they are at a barbecue, and they look genuinely happy, my dad dark from the summer, my mom light with freckles no matter the time of year. Her thick brown hair falls past her shoulders, just like mine. The photo was taken after I, their only child, left the ranch with the dream of living a life of international rivers, far from farming in the desert. And here I was on a cold linoleum floor, living the life I had dreamed of, wondering about the ranch. I didn't know what I was doing in Peru. I had felt that far-off places might help me do something great with my life, as if that were impossible in central Oregon. I rolled over, blurring my eyes on the moisture-stained ceiling in that dismal apartment, looking for inspiration. Just barely between dilated moments, the Tambopata still echoing in my ears and another river awaiting me the next day, I had nine months to go and already felt weary.

The following day, I got back to my routine. I ran two three-day Apurimac River trips a week. The Apurimac River dropped from the upper reaches of the 350-million-hectare Amazon watershed, careening through smoothed and fluted Precambrian and Paleozoic granite, a deadly river. It hammered out of the Peruvian Andes at a gradient of sixty feet per mile. There were six portages on the run that ended in massive sieves where the river could stuff a human body—and in one instance an entire sixteen-foot gear boat—underwater, between the rocks forever. The paddleboats with clients walked around those six rapids for a reason, but a guide will save his back before he saves his life. So the guides, rowing gear instead of clients, ran the portages rather than carrying the barrels, bags, coolers, boxes, and beer over a mire of rocks.

Besides being new, I was the only woman, the only non-Peruvian, and the only person who did not speak profanity-laden Spanish, and therefore I was relegated to the

gear boat and the lethal runs of the river. The canyon felt
like a coffin, and I couldn't stomach food while I was down
there. The predominately Israeli clients shat on the beaches,
never tipped, and sang obnoxious songs. The machismo in
the men I worked with tired me out. But running the portages allowed me to be alone with the river. I loved scouting
in silence and running alone. I checked the river's pulse in
those terrifyingly intimate moments when the river buried
me under aerated water.

One afternoon, after surviving another three days on the
Apurimac, I hauled my rafting gear and dry bag up the 683
stone steps from Cusco's city center to my room. My land-
lady was a dear old woman, blind, and mangled by warts
and arthritis. She never climbed the stairs to my room, but
she would meet me at the door to the street if I had a letter.
She spoke only Quechua, an ancient Andean language, but it
was clear to both of us that we adored each other. Today she
reached out for my hand, placed a letter in it, then folded my
fingers around it and smiled.

I shrugged the heavy bag with my shoulder and rushed
upstairs, spooking the one-eyed cat on the tiled roof.
Throwing my boating gear in the corner, I snuggled into my
sleeping bag, trying to insulate the heat I'd generated climbing the steps. I held the envelope in front of my face; my
Dad's squirrelly black handwriting looked familiar. I flipped
the envelope over and slipped my finger under the flap, tear-
ing it open. The paper had greasy fingerprints on either side.
I could tell that my dad had written it in the shade of the
tractor. I felt another pang of sadness for leaving him there
while I gallivanted around running rivers.

Dear Sarahlee,
I'm sad to tell you that your dear old friend,
Geraldine, passed away recently. But I got her stove
for you, because I knew you'd want it.

Geraldine Cavanah had been an old woman for as far back as I could remember. She always wore her long, gray hair in a thick braid. Her many layers of skirts and sweaters made her seem thick and warm as a mother goose. She raised sheep and goats and spun her own wool up the canyon from my family's ranch. She lived alone there in an old white farmhouse, but her son, Devereau, farmed, so he was around to give her a hand. My grandmother, Mamsy, used to take me over to her house, where I could play with sheep, needles, and dyes. I had trouble sitting still for the knitting lessons, but Geraldine persevered. She rocked forward in her chair and looked at me over her spectacles, saying, "This is an important skill for you to learn." I rocked back in my rocking chair and tried to pick up the stitches I had dropped.

Geraldine heated her old farmhouse with a small soapstone stove that the rocking chairs sat beside. Her son cussed the stove's small door, which required him to split the firewood smaller than he would have had to for any other stove. I loved it for the same reason. As a child, I could stoke the stove myself. I loved to open the door with the iron key and listen to the inferno inside. God, the thought of that stove gave me such comfort in my frigid apartment in Cusco.

Dad wrote the letter after he bought the stove. He had drawn a picture of the stove and said he'd save it for whenever I got around to building a house, because in my family that was sort of inevitable. We couldn't afford to pay anyone to do anything, so we did everything ourselves. In the meantime, he put it in the garage and set small, important machine parts on it. My fingers got cold while I read, so I reached for my gloves as I finished the letter. I was sad that Geraldine had passed away. It had been a long time since I had seen her, and I had long forgotten about her stove. Now I couldn't stop thinking about it. It seemed strange to get the letter after experiencing such a sudden shift in my feelings about home. The dry, icy air circled my face, and I blew my nose. I seemed to have a perpetual cold while I was in Cusco. I looked up through my window at the dusk-blue sky and wished I had something to eat, but instead of going back down to town for the typical fare of fried guinea pig, I fell asleep hungry.

I was out of books in English and needed something to occupy my mind, so the next day I trekked across the city to the market for fresh juice and a notebook with graph paper for sketching a house. My parents built the log house I grew up in and, on some level, I had always known I wanted to build a house at the ranch. Someday. As an old woman, probably. But in that apartment in Peru between river trips, I felt homeless, and I was beginning to realize that I couldn't build a home on writhing whitewater.

I also bought a ball of red wool yarn in honor of Geraldine and spent the afternoon knitting myself a warm hat in the only heated restaurant in town. Marco came down and met me. His leg was almost completely healed. "I'm glad you're thinking about going home," he said.

"Yeah, I think about it all the time. Too bad I won't be heading back until this time next year," I said. This would be the last time I saw Marco. He was cruising north to run the Grand Canyon, and I had a ticket the next day to Addis Ababa. I would miss him. Sharing the jungle had brought us together in a way only the jungle can. "When am I going to see you again?"

"I don't know, Shuggi. If you keep running rivers, our paths will certainly cross. But I'll probably have to find you at your ranch," he said with a smile.

I liked the sound of that. My ranch. Where people would have to find me. After ordering some variation on fried potatoes, I set to sketching. The space I'd need for living had me baffled. I couldn't remember how large a queen-size bed was, so how big did a bedroom need to be? My Peruvian apartment helped me to think small. At this time in my life, I needed a space about eight feet by eight feet. But no matter what I sketched, Geraldine's stove always held a place at the center.

For the next nine months, I hauled that little blue notebook of graph paper all over the world. From Peru, I continued around the globe, becoming more and more intimate with rivers and with myself as a person who rode them. By the time I made it back to South America and was on my way to Patagonia, the notebook was one of the few things that I'd managed to hang on to, carefully stowed away in a plastic bag, its pages nearly full.

TURNING POINT

When I turned twenty-one, I was finishing up my long year of rivers. My dream had rolled out and come to life as I started a river cleanup program in Peru, ran the longest stretch of undammed water in Africa, and worked with river protection organizations to fight dams in Costa Rica and Chile. I spent most of my time running rivers, but every river I ran had a dam proposal on it, because rivers are most vulnerable where they drop. In writhing, white rapids, I saw the earth breathing, and I breathed with it as if sitting by the side of a friend suffering from a terminal illness, one that ends in a stagnant reservoir.

The realizations I had had on the Tambopata almost a year before had stuck with me as I traveled around the world. As a child, I loved the globe that my mom gave me for my tenth birthday. I would spin it in my hands, looking at the shapes of countries, land, and sea. My fingers swept across the colorful plastic globe, guided by intense curiosity and a sort of righteousness. I didn't care about rivers then, but it was rivers that would carry me to those distant lands. That little finger on plastic was now footsteps on sand and clay, the gentle displacement of water by a boat, and contrails in the sky. The whole time, I was chased by a longing for life on a scale where I might matter. As a child, I turned the globe one way. As a woman, I turned it back. And I still had a ways to go.

My final destination of the year was the infamous Futaleufú River. I bought a van from a friend in Lima for the 3,340-mile journey south. She was a real beauty, a midnight blue Toyota diesel four-by-four. From the first hot desert grade out of the city on the Pan-American Highway with my friend Peter, we had to beat the van into running. It had become clear that the engine head was cracked, as it sputtered and blew white smoke, but it had a rockin' sound system and a bed in the back. We just added water and oil every few hours and kept driving, camping down the desert coast.

We named the van Tacna, after the Peruvian border town where we spent eleven days because I didn't have the right paperwork to get out of the country into Chile. It took us three days in first gear to cross the Atacama Desert, sometimes walking beside the van with a rock on the gas pedal. A pirated Bob Seger CD played on repeat as Tacna labored down the length of South America, with stops every other day to buy parts. What the van needed was a new engine head, but in lieu of ripping the entire engine apart, we got the little things fixed: new gaskets in Iquique, and another set in Salta. We took the temperature gauge out in Córdoba so cold water would flow through the engine constantly to keep it from overheating. Eventually Peter went his own way, and I made it to Santiago to pick up my dad for a weeklong surfing trip off the coast of Chile before my final push to Patagonia and the Futaleufú.

Dad came wobbling off the plane and out into the blaring sun as if he'd experienced some kind of time warp. I grabbed him up and held him like a precious piece of home. We headed to the coast and the town of Pichilemu, a renowned surf town. It had been a long time since we had last surfed together. We sat on our boards out beyond the breaking waves, our faces turned up to the sun, our legs dangling down into the cool water. Then he spun his board around and took three long strokes as the ocean picked him up. He stood just as the wave started to break, only his head and shoulders above the spray. He arched his back and held his arms up, his palms open like he was capturing all the energy of the sea propelling him forward. When the wave finally ran out, he fell back like he was falling into a feather bed and came up looking for me with a smile. I'd never seen anything as beautiful as my father interacting with the sea. He had a dance with it, like I had with a river, but he'd been partners with the sea much longer, and it showed.

One afternoon, while checking the surf at point breaks, Tacna developed an exhaust leak that had us leaning out the windows as we trundled along dirt tracks. We got out of the van to assess the waves through the binoculars and sat down, nauseated from diesel fumes. Back in the van, the engine temperature started to redline again, so Dad, Tacna, and I limped into a garage in Pichilemu.

I pushed in beside the mechanic to get a better look at the engine. He tapped the top of the engine with a wrench, pointing at several gaskets. I tapped the top of the engine with all five fingers and then motioned that I wanted to take the engine apart. "Tengo un grande problemo. Necesito una culata," I said in slow broken Spanish. The mechanic leaned away from me and furrowed his brow; he clearly did not like being told what to do, especially by a foreigner, and a girl to boot. We both stood silent in the door of my muddy van. The driver's seat lay behind us on the ground. I wiped my greasy hand on my only pair of pants, pulled my hair back, and waited for his verdict.

I glanced at my dad, who was perusing the walls and tables of the garage, looking at tools. He had struck up a conversation with another mechanic, asking for the words in Spanish. "Como se dice 'wrench' en Español?" He fit in well in Chile, with his indigenous Mexican features passed down from his mom's side of the family. Handsome, with silver hair against russet skin, a T-shirt in his back pocket, he was a surfer. He never wanted anything but to get away from the ranch to the beach, preferably to a Latin country. Right then, I didn't want anything but to get away from the beach, the river, South America, back to the ranch. During the year since the jungle, my direction had become clearer, even if I was still headed south instead of north.

The mechanic turned and spoke. I knew what his response would be—the same as all the others. "No, you don't need a new engine head, and we couldn't get one here in less than a month. It's not worth it to dismantle the whole engine to see. You just need new gaskets. I'll do it for two thousand pesos." I looked at the guy like he was an idiot and then walked out into the blowing dust and blaring sun to cool down. I knew the gaskets wouldn't last more than a couple of days, but what set me off was the fact that I knew better and yet over the past six months I couldn't get even one mechanic to listen to me. I didn't care if it did take a month—I couldn't get them to rip the engine apart to see. I stood there on the oil-stained dirt surrounded by old tires and the corpses of cars. Tacna was in the final stages of car cancer, and it was hard to stomach, even though she should have broken down thousands of miles before.

Dad walked up next to me, our backs to the garage. "I love this place. The mechanic said the restaurant across the street has great fish." Then he noticed my agitated look. "What's the problem? They seem nice."

I snapped my head around to look at him. "That mechanic wants to charge us ten times what new gaskets are worth, which won't even fix the problem."

"They'll fix it if they say they will—plus, the exhaust leak is what's killing us."

I looked right at him with a glare. I'd been getting ripped off for a year. "Oh, pull your head out of your ass," I said flatly.

Dad blinked and looked away. He was a good-humored guy and understood my outbursts, since he had a temper of his own. But this time something was different. "This is the stuff of dreams, Sarah." He paused for a moment. "You don't even really speak Spanish after a year down here. Why should the mechanic listen to you if you don't speak his language?" His eyes pierced me, and his lips tightened. "You're missing out on the people, Sarah. In fact," he leaned toward me, putting me in my place, "you don't even deserve to be here."

Dad turned and walked back into the garage. My tears turned into salty streaks in the hot, dry wind, which whipped my hair into the corners of my eyes. Maybe I didn't deserve to be there, but coming from the man whom I respected most and considered my best friend, those words hurt. For a moment, his reaction made me wonder if we were friends at all. I used my palms to squish the tears away, took a deep breath, and walked back into the garage where Dad was paying the mechanic. He doled his pesos out like Monopoly money.

After we ate fried fish and warm beers for lunch in silence, Tacna was ready to go. As ready as she ever would be, anyway. The mechanic looked pleased with his patch job on the exhaust pipe. The new gaskets looked a lot like the gaskets he'd replaced. But the van fired up and the fumigation didn't seem to kick in. Dad was right, the mechanic had fixed at least part of the problem and I needed to have more faith. We rolled down a potholed street, passing mostly horses and buggies instead of cars. We headed back to a point with waves that were breaking clean to the left. After suiting up in silence, we grabbed our boards and paddled out.

We finished the week together like acquaintances, all polite talk and stony faces. When Dad walked through security at the tiny Puerto Montt airstrip, all I saw was the back of his head. He didn't even turn to wave. My dad usually cried when I left for a weekend. He would follow me down the driveway on his bike as I headed to the highway, waving and weeping. He was going back to the bitter cold before farming season in the drylands of Oregon's interior, back to his film canister of rank marijuana and back to my mom, who managed an insurance office in town forty hours a week. It should have been me with a ticket in hand, elated to return to the ranch and my birthright of taking it over, but instead all I got was the back of his head and an airplane leaving me with a piece-of-shit van, lonely in my English-speaking head.

I shook it off. I had to get to the Futaleufú River. A loyal workhorse, Tacna made it across the Andes one more time.

FUTA DREAMS

Rolling into the Futaleufú River Valley in my old van, I came in on a dirt road across the high desert from the east. Foothills rose into mountains on my right and I turned and drove through them. As the land went from brown scrub to green, I pulled on my down jacket, turned on the heater, and opened my window to let the place in. Rain clouds moved over the mountaintops, still white in the early summer, dragging gauze sheets of precipitation behind them. Bob Seger's greatest hits had repeated a hundred times and were still playing when I eased out onto the Futaleufú Bridge at the Argentina border. I stopped the van right in the middle of the bridge and stepped out to see the water. The river seemed deep and unknown, folding in on itself against a short cliff, like I might go under there and come out fifty feet downstream. It felt like meeting a long-distance lover. I stepped back into the van and crossed the border into Chile, then headed to the river camp where I planned to work.

The next day I put on that aqua blue water for the first time. I leaned forward and buried my paddle when the first ice-cold wave broke over my head. The water felt hard in my eyes, nothing like the softness of my own tears, but I did not blink. I dug into the next wave face and the next. I was paddling in the bow of another guide's boat for his first run of the season. The water was running high, and a hard rain pelted the river's surface. Waterfalls blew off granite cliffs, down through the steep, temperate rainforest, and into the river. The rapids came one after another. I took the waves in the chest.

In the slow moments, my eyes searched through the dense forest that came to the water's edge. I marveled at the massive leaves and root balls. Glacier-laden peaks stood tall with their chests out on either side of the river, and the sky, upstream and down, came to the sharp point of a V. My mind was flashing home to the desert, as it was doing more and more in the deep canyons that my life flowed through. I loved this ostentatious land with its king river at the center, but the simple, distant skyline of home seemed to lie over the mountains like a transparency, cutting them in half. The boiling blue river seemed to turn to sand, and the old-growth trees squatted down into sage and rabbitbrush. The rock of the boat on the water became the long strides of my old ranch horse beneath me. That river and its valley could have outdone any other place on earth, but somehow it paled, and all I could see were the sandy canyon draws at home.

I spent another four months in Chile running Class V during the day and sketching floor plans for my house at night. I thought obsessively about the falling out with my father as I drew. Maybe he was right. When he told me I didn't deserve to be there, he meant it on a deep level. He loved water as much as I did, which was probably why rivers ran in my veins, but Dad's water was salt, and he ached for it while he circled dry fields. He was a sea person held to the land by a great anchor. And here I was, taking this endless whitewater for granted. Even the once powerful connection I'd had with whitewater had waned. In my mind, I had taken all that the river could give me, and I was ready to go home. I wanted to share that epiphany with my dad. I wanted to tell him every day why he lived in the best place on earth, that water could give only so much. That to have land, community, and history was rare.

So I drew. And in a way, though I was drawing the blueprints of a foundation for a house, I was also drawing the foundation of a relationship with my father. Somewhere on the banks of the Futaleufú, I decided that the only thing for me to do next was build. Not as an old woman, but as a twenty-one-year-old girl hoping to solve all the mysteries of my life and where I belonged. I was going to put Geraldine's stove right in the middle of the house, and Dad was the one who would help me put it there.

The rain didn't stop for most of the season, and the water stayed high. I started running my own boat and taking daily beatings on the Class V. On my last day, I climbed up on the slick log that lay in the water against the riverbank above a rapid. We could scout only the top half of it. My hair and pant cuffs were still dripping water from swimming the rapid just before. I had gotten lost in the mess of waves and holes, and suddenly I was dropped into a pit that stopped my boat, bucked it back, and threw me head over heels into the carbonated river. Shortly after I'd heaved myself onto my loose cataraft, we pulled over to scout the next one.

I looked at the entry. I had looked at it twice a week for the previous three months. I knew it by heart. Slip in to the right of the pour over at the top, snap around to the left of the rooster tail in front of the house-size boulder that the whole river slammed into, then turn and bust through a lateral wave onto a current that pushes into an uphill eddy on the right. It was the second half of the rapid that had me baffled. I would lose my left oar every time coming out of that uphill eddy, and then I'd run the bottom hole one-handed.

I ripped loose the Velcro on my pant cuffs and let the water out, cracking my knuckles and walking back to my raft to coil my bowline. I didn't feel like looking at it. Eventually the trip leader, who always ran first, put his fist in the air. I responded with a fist. He caught the downstream current and I pulled out right behind him, easing down the centerline toward the giant boulder, then slipping to the right. I dropped my head and worked to get into the eddy on the right that was pushing me out. As I dropped out of it on the downstream side, I hit a little wave askew and it ripped my left oar out of my hand and then snapped it out of the oarlock. I ignored the robbing as usual and lined up for a massive hole at the bottom that broke like a corkscrew.

The time between losing my oar and dropping into the hole always stretched into an eternity in which I just waited for the beating. To pass the time, I started singing "Angel from Montgomery" with my eye on the hole. Then the slick water sucking into the hole delivered me right into the meat of it. In less than a second I went from being on top of the hole to looking up at the wave breaking like a massive open palm. It reached up and grabbed my boat. I grabbed my frame as the boat went over backward.

In that instant, my legs dangled down into a seam between two violent currents. I held my breath and held onto the frame. Looking up, I could see aerated white, but I could hear nothing. I was enveloped in true, perfect silence, a liquid cold that I could feel on every surface of my body. Suddenly, my legs came free and I burst up, gasping for air. Heaving myself into the raft, I glanced upstream, looking for that sneaky wave that had taken my oar and sent me swimming for the second time that day.

We drifted downstream to the takeout and loaded the boats. I put my wet gear on the bus and ran the nine miles back to camp. My feet felt good on solid ground, weaving down the gravel road as I tried to avoid the washboard. It was my last day in the Futaleufú Valley. I stopped on the footbridge to stretch and look downstream. I was on my way back to the desert, and I stood there wishing every river in the world flowed through the ranch so I wouldn't have to choose. But instead, the ranch was dry, and we were piping our seasonal canal. There was more than the end of a season in that last glimpse of the Futaleufú: red peaks shrouded in cloud, a splash of light across their chests, yellowed willows along the banks of a darkened river. I had to walk away from my affair with that canyon and its whitewater.

My heart broke to think that I might never see it run again, that a reservoir might bury it before I could get back. It was like leaving a lover, walking away, and then turning to see if he's still watching, waving. But I knew where I needed to be. I needed the desert, my family, a community. In that moment, looking down at the water swirling beneath me, I wondered what kind of love I must have for the ranch if it wasn't like that for a lover. Perhaps a deeper love, like that for a grandmother. I wondered if I would always miss the chemistry of that fling with the river. I felt crazy for leaving something so good, but I guess it was like any fling—I just couldn't imagine it being enough to sustain me forever. And though I loved to play, I'd been missing real work, in a real place, with real people who work the land. By this time, I'd been homesick for what felt like a decade. And I was done accepting that low-grade ache. I was ready to try a new solution besides running away from it, always downstream. As much as I wanted the mystique of *river runner*, I was so clearly a child of the high desert, of a particular piece of ground, and I couldn't deny that anymore. Though it would be hard to leave the river, I would have my horse to carry me as I searched for a balance between rivers and the ranch.

That night, the sky cleared and the temperature dropped. When I stumbled out of my van to pee, I stood and watched the river lift out of itself into a soft white stream that floated up and settled around the necks of the mountains like a giant feather boa. The quivering stars on the black glass surface sank away into the white haze, and before I knew it, the river's ghost was overhead.

The next day I headed north to Santiago, where I could

buy a plane ticket. After making it through Argentina and over the Andes, Tacna puttered to a dead stop outside Puerto Varas, a couple of days' drive short of Santiago. I couldn't bring myself to go to another mechanic. I dumped my river life there on the side of the road. I left the van for the scavengers, hitched a ride to Santiago, and flew home. Why it took me a year to have such conviction I do not know, but I knew it then, and I was gone.

RIVERS FLOW TOWARD HOME

R ivers had run over and through my body, and in the end
they delivered me to the place I least expected. From
the international airport in Portland, it's a three-hour drive
to my family's ranch in central Oregon. At the summit point
of the Oregon Cascades, I headed east and broke away to
my high-desert home. It was a year after the Tambopata
and *Walden*. The land in front of me looked like a massive
cupped hand, the Three Sisters Mountains its fingertips and
the Crooked and Deschutes rivers its lifelines. Dropping
down through the burnt ponderosa forest, I took a shortcut
through the meadows at Indian Ford to the top of a sand
and rimrock canyon where I eased into the familiar muted
colors of the juniper forest. I slowed where the road bent
back on itself, past where a pair of golden eagles perch. As I
circled around the north slope of the rimrock that contains
our valley, the bright green fields at Long Hollow Ranch

opened onto the western reaches of what I like to call the Lower Bridge Valley. Where the canyon slope makes a hard turn to the south, the road jogs left alongside my family's ranch, and our whole world was laid out in front of me. This was my country, where the land gets big and I can see two mountain ranges in the distance, fields nestled between buttes and rimrock dotted with juniper. The irrigation canal ran half full under the road. Two cuttings' worth of hay stood in stacks outside our old potato cellar, waiting for me to haul the bales by hand through the low doors. Dad's old red Chevy sat by the tractor on the far side of the field. I honked, and he threw an arm up.

My windows open wide to the summer, I pulled into the driveway and stopped for a moment to take in this long-awaited homecoming. A part of me was nervous that maybe it wouldn't be what I had remembered or hoped. I was afraid it wouldn't feel like home, and that I would have given up so much and come so far to realize the river really was where I was supposed to be. The ranch seemed to absorb all life, events, and labor in a way that made it timeless. Over a year ago, the place had looked exactly the same, except I had been looking at it in my rearview mirror. The haying equipment had been moved to the fields from where it waited out the winter beside the driveway. My black gelding grazed in the green field of crested wheat behind the three-pole jack fence braced on hardpan. Mamsy and Bompa, my father's parents, stood on the north deck of their log house, framed by Mamsy's prized geraniums. This was a family ranch, and I smiled as I recalled my last image of them standing there, one I had held close through my travels.

I eased up the driveway and into the low spot where my parents had built their house, hidden from the road and wind. My mom had nestled us in there, planting flowerbeds, vegetable gardens, and aspens like soft blankets to keep the desert at bay. Irises bloomed in the shifting light beneath the trees, and tomatoes ripened against the south wall of their log house. She worked in town all week and wouldn't be home until later. I marveled at her gardens and ate a warm tomato, the juice dripping down my arm.

On the north shoulder of the ranch, behind my parents' house, was our small hay field, where Dad lapped tractors pulling hay equipment while he watched the world go by. Two long rural roads came to a junction at the corner of the hay field, making it seem like a sort of hub. Reaching out to the metal gate, I let my head fall back to look up through the gnarled limbs of an old juniper tree. The desert summer sun warmed the backs of my legs instantly when I moved out of the tree's shadow and up to the edge of the field. Fluffed, green windrows stretched down the field, and Dad bounced slowly toward me on the tractor, monitoring the baler behind him. I waited for him at the top of the field, looking east.

This was central Oregon, on the edge of some of the West's vastest wild deserts, far from the soggy cities to the west. Our farm rested at the wide mouth of McKenzie Canyon, and I imagined the massive flood that would have deposited our field, an alluvial fan blasting out onto the shoulders of the drainage. From the top of the field I could feel the ultimate movement of this land, eroding toward the Deschutes River for its ride to the Columbia and eventually the sea, my dad tumbling along with it. An unfurled juniper forest drenched in golden late-afternoon light ran up the sides of distant buttes and bristled their flat tops. I breathed deep through my nose, pulling in the smell of fresh-cut hay, warm juniper, and dust. For the first time, the most familiar view wasn't just *there*, it was beautiful. Perfect.

Rivers and the journey they had taken me on—not only through canyons but also through life—haunted me even then, standing in the field. I was afraid of what my dad would say. All I could think about was the last time I had seen him, walking away. And the possible rejection of what I had decided was the only right thing for me to do.

He dropped the RPMs on the tractor, took it out of gear, and stepped down. I took him in my arms and spoke over his shoulder. "So. What do you think?" Mom had already mentioned my idea.

He didn't respond immediately, so I held on, bending to nestle my head under his wide-brimmed straw hat. I looked down at his dark red back, at the tan lines from the straps of his overalls. The breeze shifted my hair and long shadows grew down the field as the day cooled. The baler pumped behind the tractor, its ram thrusting through the chamber at a slow beat. The grass at our feet was short, and the hay bales behind us emerald green.

"I'll be there if you are, but I won't do it for you. You have to lead." His words were slow and deliberate, and I felt my face pull into a smile against his shoulder.

BREAKING GROUND

At the end of a long farming season, Mom and I grabbed a couple of shovels and a pick from where they leaned against the north side of my parents' house. We headed northwest to the center of the property, to the exact site where I wanted to build. Our land was a long rectangle that ran from a rimrock on the western boundary down to Lower Bridge Road on the east. Three-quarters of the land was dry ground where we kept horses and cattle, depending on the year. Our barn sat at the northern edge along Holmes Road, near our irrigation ponds and just above the quarter of our property that has irrigation rights. We watched Dad circle the hay field that sat at the corner of Lower Bridge and Holmes as we walked out of sight of their house and the field, across a rocky clearing and into a juniper thicket on a slight rise.

As a child I liked to sit and read poetry with Mamsy under the biggest, oldest juniper tree near my site. Where the Cascade Mountains marked west, I loved the dry spring creek, and just beyond there, the old homestead where I collected bits of green and blue glass, rusty tin cans and gooseberries. I found the best arrow heads in the sand there. I pretended I was a pioneer in a wagon train on the old wagon road between Prineville and Sisters. The deep grooves, worn one hundred years before, ran just to the north of my spot. Beyond that, the seasonal irrigation ditch flowed into a pond rippling with frog song. I played there on the grassy banks when the water slowed to a trickle in summer.

As a returning adult, I looked at the place with a more practical eye. The slight southern slope felt nestled into the land, backed by a dense juniper thicket to curtail the prevailing wind. The structure I planned would face south and slightly west, every window placed for streaming light, passive solar gain, and a splendid view. The roof would have multiple aspects to take full advantage of solar power panels and a solar hot-water heater. Though the ground sloped and would be somewhat difficult to build on, the angle would allow a simple gray-water system out front, enough to support a small greenhouse. Three hundred and seventy steps from the house I grew up in, it felt just far enough these days.

Mom and I dug holes to assess the ground at the building site. I found about three inches of dirt in most places before I hit hardpan.

"Am I supposed to dig down into this?" I said as I chipped at the ground with my shovel.

"Well, the deeper the better. You have to get below the frost line." Mom laughed at my dejected look. "You could rent a backhoe."

"I want to do it myself," I mumbled and sat down.

"Let's go get the tractor to clear these little trees," Mom said, giving me the motivation I needed.

Hesitantly, I pulled six small trees to open up space for building. Their roots splayed out like long, slender fingers and toes. Where the roots were stripped they showed red, like skin filled with blood. Their roots looked like giant hoop skirts, having traveled out along the hardpan in just three inches of dirt. They were easily as long as the tree was tall. Huge circles of bare rock were left when I pulled them out. I left as many trees as I could, including an ancient one not five feet from the corner of the house and a row of them not far from what would be the north wall. They would be in the way of the log work, but trees seemed worth the trouble.

The sky was the color of lemon cream and the northwest slopes of the Sisters caught the last sun as I pulled my little blue book out of my pocket and opened it to the most recent sketch of my house. It was shaped like a fat *T*, with a forty-foot back wall, a twenty-foot front wall, and forty-foot sidewalls that would jog in ten feet at their midpoint—a 1,200-square-foot floor plan. The shape came from a need for shorter walls, and therefore shorter, straighter, and cheaper logs. The size came from my careful estimation of the space I would need for basic living. Central Oregon was bloating with wealth and places that looked like nursing homes, mansions built for two people to enjoy a view on the weekend; I was making a conscious choice to live differently.

After following the summer shadows of the big juniper trees in front of my house site, Mom and I set our first stake at the northwest corner. We used the rule of triangulation to set the other corners square with the first. We fumbled with the hundred-foot measuring tape, rechecking our points several times for absolute accuracy. This must have been so familiar to her, scratching out a spot on the desert to try to make a life. She had certainly inspired me. I wonder if she looked across that little piece of bare ground and saw herself in me. Tossing a rock out of the plot, I had her same broad shoulders and hips, long braid, blue jeans, and dusty boots. Not to mention a staunch determination to do something without knowing how, at least in the traditional sense. I guess the rationale is: if it can be done, I can do it.

Mom was glad to help me whenever she could until Dad finished farming. Having me close and clearly invested in the ranch and our family made her happier than anyone, especially since I was talking like I might stay forever. We strung thin white twine taut between the stakes. I stepped back and smiled at the lines, faint tracings on my sketchboard of land. Squinting just right, I could see the shadow of my house.

The next morning I walked up to my spot, shuffling through the dust and weeds, shovel in hand. To my left, the Cascades didn't even have a thin shawl of snow. The whole North Sister stood bare. Not a patch of snow was left at the end of summer, and the Canada geese already grazed in the field. When I rounded the big juniper tree to gaze at my sketch, it was gone. Broken stakes and strings festooned the sagebrush. I gasped. As I moved closer, I found hundreds of horse prints and two piles of manure. My site was in the center of the horses' grazing, so I should have expected curiosity. Of the forty horses, I knew exactly which horse had done the damage. I imagined Vince carefully dismantling the strings, then loping off with a snicker.

I set my shovel down and marched back to the house for fencing supplies. The horses had eighty acres to themselves and, whether they liked it or not, I was going to take one of those acres for myself. After replacing my strings, I drove metal posts into the ground and stretched two smooth wires around my site. I placed an iron bar through the middle of the wire roll so I could unravel it, but the roll bounced and jerked against my leg. By the end of the day my thighs were black and blue. I wondered when my dad was going to help me. It seemed like every little thing would be infinitely easier with two people, and as one person I couldn't believe how painful this process already was. I was running my palms lightly over my thighs when my neighbor stopped by to comment on my initial efforts.

"Don't break yourself down on the fence before you start to build," he cautioned. "Thanks, Glen. I wish you'd shown up sooner to tell me that."

Glen was seventy that year. He had lived at the end of the road for forty-two years, but he was originally from California, which he kept a secret. He wasn't like all the other Californians looking for more space, and in doing so, filling in all the space. He reminded me that he'd been in the valley twice as long as I had even though I was born there. He had to borrow five hundred dollars for gas to get here in 1964. Now he stood there in his jeans and jean jacket, glasses pocked from running his welder, a wisp of white hair peeking out from under his billed hat. He poked around for a minute, then walked back to his truck. No doubt he was on his way to spread rumors of my naiveté.

That fenced acre in the middle of eighty acres reminded me of the square-foot plots we were assigned as fourth graders. On the empty lot next to the Terrebonne grade school, we put a little piece of white string around our assigned spots, held in place by toothpicks. I sat and studied that little plot for science class. Over the course of a year, I learned about the sandy loam soil and the cheatgrass, and watched grasshoppers and ants move through. The plot in front of me now was a bit bigger, but I planned to study it just the same.

A year in the same place, spent outside and generally alone, required a puppy. The malamute I'd grown up with had passed on and my parents wanted another big dog at the ranch, so I picked the biggest male out of a litter of German shepherd/lab mixes. I liked that he slept at the back of the pen while the other puppies whined and jumped and bit. He waited in the truck while I picked up some puppy food, and then we drove home in time to change the irrigation at midday. He chased me around the short-grass field with a "don't leave me" look in his eyes, and I called him Chyulu after the hills close to where I had lived in Kenya.

Back at the home site, he conked out in the dirt while I dug the first leg of my foundation. Forty feet. My pickax chipped at the hardpan, every strike a tinny rejection, exertion slammed back into my hands, arms, and back. I thought about using a backhoe, but I just wanted to be in my space, getting the job done as I could do it with my own body.

Chyulu didn't care. As long as he could hear me working, he was happy to snooze in a pile of dirt.

In the afternoon, Dad toodled up on his yellow and red bike after baling. He squatted next to the puppy and woke him up with a nudge under the chin. They made eye contact, and then Chyulu flopped back over. Dad grabbed his old shovel with the duct tape flaking off the handle and helped clear the hardpan I chipped with the pickax and crowbar. "How are we going to do the concrete for the foundation?" he asked while he let me get ahead. This was the first time he had been up to the site, and he'd worked hard to get there after a long day on the tractor. When he arrived, he knew what to do.

I stopped for a second, smiling at the man this was all for. It was as if he'd stepped into my notebook and my dreams were coming true. I wondered if I should apologize for what happened in Chile, but Dad always said to move on, that there wasn't any time for looking back. Then I considered the concrete. "I really just want to mix and pour it by hand." All I could imagine was the frenzy around a concrete truck. What if the forms blew out and we couldn't move fast enough and the concrete started to go off? The driver would just pour it out in a pile. A big concrete pile of failure. "I would just rather take it slow."

"Sounds like a lot of work. Maybe you should look into it," he said, clearing the chipped earth out of the ditch. And that was all. We worked like that until the sun went down.

Everyone had an opinion. One friend recommended posts and beams on pier pads for the foundation. It sounded great, quick, easy, and sufficient. He worried that my stem wall would be weak from the incongruity of many pours, but more importantly, that the work would be so difficult that I would burn out at the ground level. I understood that he wanted to save me frustration, but what he told me threw me into a paroxysm. I was sure that my house would stick up like a sore thumb on a makeshift foundation until it eventually fell over.

I decided to ask a pro, so I called Central Oregon Log Homes to find out if I could build a log home on pier pads. The office gave me the cell number of the general contractor. Chain saws whined in the background when he answered his phone and yelled, "Hello!"

"Mr. Moon? Excuse me, but do you know about building a log home on pier pads?" He paused, no doubt confused. "No."

I thanked him and got back to pricing sand, gravel, Portland cement, and a mixer. I was willing to take advice, but in the end I had to keep plowing through life on my own, doing things the way they made sense to me. As a mild fall turned to a bitter winter, this process became typical for all the stages of house construction: concrete, floor, logs, roof, windows, and doors. First, I had to research the many different ways to do any part of the construction. Then I compared prices and opinions and time. Eventually I could decide on a plan of attack. Next, I amassed the tools and materials for the task. Then I learned how to use them. When I finally felt comfortable with the task, I would start the next phase of the project. It was an exhausting cycle, and I longed for the day when I would step out the door in the morning and know how to do whatever I had to do that day.

IN FRONT OF A WINTER EVENT

A few loose hairs fell in front of my headlamp's light and narrowed my focus like lightning in the dark. Digging and pouring my foundation, I worked through a range of light. From morning light to broad daylight to flat light to low-angle light—warm late-afternoon light, shifting light through shadows, no light, headlamp light, quarter-moon light, half-moon light, full-moon light. Day nineteen: the wind blew hard as I poured the stem wall around the southeast corner. I mixed and poured concrete into the dark, determined to finish the corner. That evening, I walked back to my parents' house with heavy steps, exhausted. I hung my head, my eyes focused on the ground in front of me, and the jingle of Chyulu's tags followed me as I crawled through the horse fence. The lights of Bend and Redmond glowed orange on the underbellies of dense clouds, and seemed brighter than ever—encroaching light pollution. I labored up the two

steps into the mudroom and smelled the savory scent of dinner and wood smoke. I pulled off my boots and left them
tidily at the end of the line of boots. Dad sat low on the old
milking stool in front of the woodstove. He was lighting it
for the first time since April; winter loomed. Mom pulled my
dinner plate out of a warm oven, and I thanked her for saving me some food.

My forearms and wrists ached. I had bruises along the
sides of my thighs from carrying buckets of sand and gravel.
I had bruises on the inside of my left forearm from pulling
the bucket with my right arm and throwing my left under it
to dump the four shovelfuls of mix into the concrete mixer.
My fingers split, and I knew the cement dust couldn't be
good for me, but wearing a dust mask made my face sweat
and itch. I hoped my body and my poor old concrete mixer
would make it back around to the northwest corner of the
foundation where we started. Maybe another week? Maybe
more. When I fell asleep I dreamt that the concrete crumbled, twisted, and threw itself down the south slope.

The next morning, Mom climbed up the half-finished
stairs to my room. We had moved into our house when I
was in seventh grade, after a decade of house building in
the evenings while my parents worked full-time jobs. The
house wasn't completely done at the time, but my room was
painted and had carpet and I had begged to move in. Mom
didn't want to move in before the house was completely
done, because she knew she'd never finish it after that. And
indeed, the stairs, among other things, remained unfinished.

She walked lightly into my room and sat on the edge of
my bed. Chyulu and I were sleeping back to back and she

reached over me to scratch his belly. Then she turned off my bedside light, which had been on all night, pulled my journal out from under my face, and laughed at the ink marks on my cheek. "Your eggs are ready," she said, and I heard the squeak of the top stair as she went back down to the kitchen.

I pulled back my hair, which had gotten too long, slid into my robe, and eased my aching body down the stairs. Squinting across the room at the weather map on the TV, I noticed a storm front out in the Pacific. The weatherman smirked as he pointed to the storm, "One last window of decent weather will likely close in five days."

"Damn, Dad, this has taken longer than I thought it would," I said.

"Yeah, if we had gotten a concrete truck, we would have been done in a day instead of three weeks," he said, a little irritated.

"Come get your eggs," Mom called from the kitchen.

Suddenly in a hurry, I wolfed down my eggs, jumped into my sweatshirt, jeans, and boots, and ran out the back door. I was determined to finish within that window of weather, or my whole project would be on hold until spring. Even so, November was late in the season to be pouring concrete. You can't pour concrete in freezing temperatures, because the chemicals in the cement heat up when mixed with water, and in cold weather they can't get hot enough to harden. But without a foundation, I couldn't start putting up the logs.

Dad joined me at the house site after he had fed the horses and his chickens and shoveled Chyulu's poo off the lawn. He thought I should be doing that job, but let it go for the time being.

"Only fools make dreams with dates," Dad said as he shoveled concrete into the forms we'd set up the day before, "At least we haven't started working backward yet."

Dad's comment fell on deaf ears. I continued to shovel frantically, and silently. I had been skipping meals, chores, and sleep. It took six hours to mix four bags of cement, which made about twenty wheelbarrow loads. Each load required four buckets of sand and gravel, a half bucket of cement, and a long squirt with the hose. I spent all my daylight hours counting, figuring how much cement I had, how long each batch took, how much time I had, how far I could get.

At the end of the day, I drove four miles to our hay barn at the end of the gravel road. On top of pouring the foundation, I delivered my dad's hay to customers, three tons at a time, to pay for the cement, sand, and gravel. I liked the drive when the radio worked and I got to listen to country music. I saw our neighbors in their fields and barns working late, too. I loaded my trailer every evening to deliver the next morning. That evening, when the weatherman predicted that winter was hot on our heels, I got my truck stuck in the mud at the barn and had to walk home. I wasn't surprised or even mad. It reminded me that when I didn't think I had an extra second in the day, the day would give me one.

After the wheels spun once, I locked the truck, put on my jacket, and walked to the road. The walk was just what I needed—time to move easily without lifting and straining. To think about what Dad had said about making dreams with dates. I worked as hard as I could, with unwavering focus. Maybe an enlightened person would plug away gracefully, not wasting time or energy on stress. Work smarter, not harder, they say. But at times like these, when something out of your control bears down, it's time to dig deeper and stretch yourself far beyond any rational limit. The same determination that kept me from drowning on some remote river would get my foundation poured.

The next morning the weatherman smirked again—not only was the window closing, but it would be closed by a "serious winter event." At 7:00 a.m. we finished the last wheelbarrow loads of concrete and poured the foundation to the northwest corner. Laying twenty yards of concrete by hand had been a journey like no other. After we cleaned the tools, Dad patted me on the back and we watched the storm stack up behind the Cascades. The mountains were clear then, backed by black.

"This is the stuff of dreams, Sarah. One giant hurdle closer to a house." Dad grabbed a concrete blanket and threw it over the last section we'd poured.

I had heard him say this before—the stuff of dreams—when we were in Chile, referring to very different "stuff." But he knew this was my dream, and that's why he worked by my side, allowing me to do it in my own way. "Thanks, Dad," I said and turned to him.

He put his arms around me, and I bent my limp arms at my elbows to put my hands against his back. I laid my head on his shoulder and breathed into the heavy canvas hug. I felt so lucky to have a dad who would give up six months to help his daughter fulfill a dream. Even if a dad wanted to, most could not afford the time.

"You never back down," he said as he let go.

When I was a child, my dad did not hold my hand or protect me from small dangers. He let me fall and he let me pull myself back up, brushing the dirt off myself. I drained and coiled the long hose I had strung up from my parents' house. "And what a dramatic finish," I said as we moseyed home for an early lunch. His admiration was rare and made me feel like I had passed a test, and would be allowed to go on.

Within hours, the storm swallowed up the mountains. No telling when they'd be back. The land lost its color and the ceiling dropped. The closest rimrock became the farthest distance I could see. The winter of 2005 to 2006 had officially arrived. I suppose it could have arrived when the last poplar leaf fell. Or the day I woke up and all the horses had their winter coats on. But those events could be considered late fall. That day, winter arrived in its sure, quiet, snow-insulated way, and I promised myself I wouldn't just be waiting for spring. I looked forward to log work in the snow and endless time with my father.

GROWING UP

In Terrebonne, the town I am from, kids grow up and stay. Girls end up pregnant and boys die driving drunk. I grew up with one friend at the end of the road. Jessica Ellison loved babies, baking, horses, and boys. As kids, Jess and I both had chores and a horse, and we didn't play sports. She couldn't wait to have a family, while I daydreamed about riding horses across Africa and Mongolia. She wanted a house and I wanted the world, but we were best friends.

My mother won the state arm-wrestling championship in 1978 and moved ten tons of hay the day I was born. She always said, "Sixteen is too young to be a mom," and had waited until she was thirty, agreeing reluctantly to have just one child after my father begged for months. There was a hole in the middle finger of her work gloves from grabbing at the strings of hay bales. Her thick auburn hair hung halfway down her back, and she let it down when she went to town. She sewed up the knees in my jeans and the deep cuts in the horses' hides when they ran through the barbed wire fence. Her philosophy on mothering was one of release: a bow that shoots an arrow into the world. A tall, slim woman with strong, callused hands, my mom was needed everywhere and stepped into many shoes with ease and a gentle voice. I've never seen her cry.

A big woman with long, dark hair, Jessica's mother had the smothering quality of a mama bear. Her family locked their doors, unlike most people I knew, and the key was under the can of sage rat poison in the storeroom. We were told to hide in the upstairs closet whenever anyone drove up. As a kid, the story I heard was something about Jessica's mom spending some time in jail because she'd gotten mixed up in a robbery and the hostage had a heart attack in the trunk of her car and died. I didn't know what to believe, but Jess seemed to believe that her mom couldn't get a job because any employer would do a background check and she'd lose the kids. Jessica and her brother seemed captive on the farm. They worked, hid, and were homeschooled.

Jessica drove an old yellow Dodge pickup. I tore around in a lifted, battleship-gray Ford with the paint peeling off the hood. We were eleven and twelve. One day, we were supposed to be loading my truck with hay, but as we approached the public land turnoff I glanced at Jess and she smiled. She didn't have to say anything. I barely hit the brakes and took the corner. The back tires slung mud as we swerved through the gate. We loved to go muddin'.

We didn't get far before the left tire dropped off the narrow track and the truck tipped over onto its side. It landed softly in the mud, choked, and died when I slammed the brake to the floor without pushing in the clutch. We sat there silently for a moment before bursting into nervous laughter. It took both of us to open Jess's door against gravity so we could climb out. We ran a mile across our neighbor's deep-disked field and forced ourselves to tears so her dad would take pity on us. There certainly wasn't a reason for us to be anywhere but the barn, so weeping was our only defense. It worked.

We lived on hay farms, so we spent summer days moving hay and changing irrigation pipes. Summer in the desert brings all things to the color of dust, and we were no exception. We slipped out of the dust like superheroes from phone booths, leaving a thin film on the surface of the pond when we jumped off the slick pump platform. As summer wore on, the pond sucked down and our floating island dock came to rest on the bank, a haven for giant toads. In the afternoons, we saddled up our horses. I had a big black gelding that was as explosive as a powder keg. Jessica rode a bay horse that was lame most of the time. Our favorite trail was the old wagon road by the burnt-out homestead cabin with the fallen juniper tree covered in neon-green moss. That green was the only vibrant thing on the desert. In the evenings we sketched barn plans and dreamed we would train beautiful Andalucian horses and grow old together.

Jessica and I carved our names on either side of the letters *BFF* (best friends forever) in the young aspen tree outside my bedroom window the day her parents let her ride the bus to school for the first time. She loved the week of middle school home economics when we had to carry a large bag of flour everywhere we went, practicing to be moms. She put a dress on hers. I put duct tape around mine, but when I was running my horse down to the river it fell out of the sling on my back, erupting into a white cloud in the trail behind me. Even now, a baby will inevitably start wailing the second I touch it. There was no doubt in my adolescent mind that being a mom would kill me. Jess was ready, though, even in middle school.

Jessica and I enjoyed only one year at school together before her mom sent her to a Christian school. Then we went back to hanging out on the weekends like we had when she was homeschooled. Jess had a tiny room in the south end of the attic with a little single-paned window that twisted with intricate frost in the wintertime. We were sitting on the floor, leaning against her bed, when Jess told me she had seen an angel vanish behind a beanpole tree that grew along the sidewalk in the city. I thought to myself that Christian school was making her talk about strange things, but I said I believed her. I guess that wasn't good enough, because she left a letter in my mailbox saying we couldn't be friends because we couldn't agree about something as simple as God. I know now that there is nothing simple about God, let alone angels and beanpole trees, but that was the day the road forked.

Jessica devoted herself to God, while I reared and bucked and pulled against my reins looking for a way to get out of central Oregon. I hated Redmond High School and felt isolated at the end of the road, at the end of an hour-and-a-half school-bus ride. One evening, my dad passed me his copy of *Surfer* magazine with an article about New Zealand in it.

"Check this out, Sar, they say you can surf and snow-board in the same day," he said and reached over to point out one of the pictures.

Dad had spent several months there in his twenties and declared the place paradise. I looked at the pictures and couldn't think of anything cooler.

"You're getting pretty good at snowboarding, and you always wanted to get better at surfing," he said. "And I'd sure come to visit!"

With my parents' support, I researched and saved to spend my junior year abroad as an exchange student. They believed anything is possible if a person puts their mind to it, and I was a product of that belief.

While I was living in Canterbury Plains, New Zealand, a letter from Jessica Clark arrived. I didn't recognize the name, but the tiny, loopy handwriting looked familiar. I hadn't talked to Jessica in years. She wrote to tell me she'd gotten pregnant and married the cute blonde boy at her Christian school. I was not surprised. I don't think they had sex education at the Christian school. I heard they told girls that if they abstained, they might go to heaven. In public school, they scared us out of sex with terrifying talk about AIDS, herpes, and pregnancy. I had watched Jess get swallowed by the gut of our small town where the 7-Eleven squats on the north side of Highway 20, where good Christian girls take their tops off and give blow jobs to hicks in big trucks.

Jess never got to wear the strapless dress that billowed into a princess gown at her wedding. There was no baby's breath in her hair and no bouquet of wild purple lilies from the desert in the springtime. I think they just went to the courthouse. She said she was envious of my travels, but she wanted to ride horses when I got home at Christmas.

When I got home, I was nervous to see Jessica after so long, but I figured our history would bridge time and experience.

She had given birth to a baby boy, Brian, by the time I got home, so we couldn't ride together. For the first time in years, I drove to Prineville, where she and her husband lived. The town was at the heart of central Oregon's redneck contingent and sat to the east of my family's ranch. To the south, Bend was overrun with yuppie hippies. To the west, Sisters thrived with retired, quilting folks. And to the north, Madras sustained the Mexicans and Indians. Our ranch was smack in the middle, slightly insulated by a river, farm ground, and public land.

Jessica lived in her husband's grandmother's house. Gramma had died recently. When I pulled up, the house was dark, with one string of lights out front. I knocked and walked in. There was a foot of snow on the ground outside, and it wasn't any warmer in the house. Jess was sitting in the dark with Brian and turned on a lamp next to the couch.

"Hi, Sarah. Welcome home."

I left my jacket on and took a seat. "How are you?"

"Well, I'm finally a mom," she spoke softly as she looked down at her baby, but her expression wasn't as tender as I thought it would be. She cut right to the chase. "It isn't what I expected."

I wasn't sure what she meant. Wasn't she living her dream?

"Everyone expects you to love your own child, but I don't even feel like I know him."

I didn't know what to say. I looked around the room. It looked camped in, with the one couch and a small pile of things against the wall. No pictures on the walls, no baby paraphernalia.

"Want to go to Dairy Queen?" she asked.

"Sure."

"My husband will be off work soon; he can meet us there." She stood and picked Brian up. He cried and wouldn't stop even when she held him close. We didn't have to bundle up, because we already were. We took short, careful steps out to the old yellow Dodge pickup. Our childhood came flooding back to me as I pulled myself up into the passenger seat. I tried to remember Jess the way she used to be, but it was tough. She plopped Brian flat in the center seat and shut the door. There wasn't any excitement about going for a drive, no silly banter. The truck choked on the cold, but fired up. We idled for a minute, the exhaust billowing around us on that perfectly still winter night.

At the DQ, we ordered Tater Tots and soft ice cream. Under the bright lights I noticed a bruise on her cheekbone, back by her ear. I didn't say anything.

"So, how was New Zealand?" she asked with a sweet, forced smile.

"Good, ya know. I really enjoyed the mountains," I responded, but felt odd talking about my grand adventures.

Her husband showed up after he got off work at the Quickie Lube. He plopped down on the red vinyl seat next to Jessica and Brian. The baby started to cry, and he leaned over the boy and yelled, "Shut up!" The only other people in the restaurant stared for a moment, whispering. Jess looked at her lap. I dipped a Tater Tot in ketchup and held my tongue.

The summer after my freshman year at college, I was guiding on the Arkansas River in Colorado. A letter came from Jessica Ellison. She said she'd divorced that wife-beater husband and had custody of Brian. She said her son was enough man for her. She had a steady job at the hospital and lived in a nice apartment in Redmond. When I got home to see her, her kid was beautiful and so was she, her hair long and reddish brown. She had finally gotten her braces off. She was thin, and her skin was clear and fair.

The next summer, I worked at a ranch on an African veldt of whistling thorn that clutched the northern slopes of Mount Kenya and dropped into the Great Rift Valley—a horizon like the sea. I had been there for six months, breaking horses. After a long day of delivering food stores with camels to cattle herdsmen scattered over fourteen thousand acres, I found a letter from my mother.

> *Dear Sarah,*
> *I have thought a lot about telling you this before you get home, but I think you should know. Jessica was at a party and passed out. A guy threw her over his shoulder. He tripped and dropped her on her head in the parking lot. She died later that evening. I went to the funeral and took some desert lilies, because I know you would have liked to.*
>
> > *Love,*
> > *Mom*

I sat on the shady veranda of the old brick ranch house amid a wild garden exploding with color and exotic fruits. My eyes fell out of focus. I'd never experienced a human death, especially the death of someone who essentially could have been me. Home was supposed to be safe, a place where people could grow old and bored. She missed her twenty-first birthday by a month. I realized I had been in another country for anything that had ever happened in my best friend's short lifetime, and I wasn't sure if I'd let her down, saved my life, or both. To me, Jessica died along with something of my childhood. I didn't cry. I made apple crumble in her honor and rode in silence. A great herd of giraffes towered over me like a cathedral that day.

I can't always remember a face, but I can remember a laugh. The winter I spent building my house was the first time I'd been home since Jess's death, and I wallowed through the snow that Glen, my neighbor, said was more than he could ever remember. The lifted Ford still had paint flaking off the hood, and I was using it to move eighty tons of hay on my own when I wasn't working on the house. I plugged away at my hay delivery side business and had to dig into the barn for each load. Every day, I passed by the old white farmhouse where Jessica used to live. I remembered its smell of greasy farm cooking. Now, the windows were boarded up and the driveway was full of snow. I thought of Jess on those bitterly cold days, when icicles dangle off the horses' whiskers and bellies and chinkle when they trot. When I passed the aspen tree on the way to the chicken coop, I paused to find our mark. The letters *BFF* had stretched and distorted over the years.

Sometimes I imagine Jessica's entire life scattered in the sagebrush, flung out in front of me like the tiny yellow flowers that blanket the desert when the ground thaws in the spring. Jess's short lifetime, like those yellow flowers, had gotten me down on my belly to look closely, to reflect on the amount of living a person can do before she turns twenty-one, or twenty-three in my case. I wondered if leaving home had saved my life—after all, Jess and I grew up out of the same high desert hardpan, and that was where she ended up. Now I had ended up there as well, though not as a premature ending—as a beginning. But if I was the arrow shot from a powerful bow, the black cotton soils of Africa, the orange dust of Colorado, and the alluvial plains of New Zealand had nurtured me. If I hadn't experienced the world, digging into the hardpan would be different. Before, I would have believed it could hold a body, but I don't think I could have trusted it to hold my roots. Now, no other place in the world was up to the task.

BEAVER DAMS

My dad says I was first introduced to the enormity of logs before I turned two. I stood in my crib in the old yellow farmhouse, drenched in the bright light of a west-facing window next to me. Wood smoke hovered and burned my nose. Through this window—trimmed in thin metal, with dead flies on the sill—I watched my father outside. Sometimes intricate patterns of ice formed on the glass, and through it I once saw Dad turn his calloused hand over, his fingers wide on the glass, tracing waves in the thin layer of ice with his nails.

One morning, Dad was carving on an upright juniper log. The log was a couple of feet taller than him, and just about as big around. He had it leaned against the house and was teasing out the figure of a woman with his chain saw. He stopped for a moment to look at me, his saw dangling in one hand by his side as he adjusted his safety glasses. Then, suddenly, the log fell, pummeling him out of my view. I didn't cry immediately, but I clutched the rails of my crib. The single pane of glass was hazy and the light so bright that when my father disappeared, I could see only white. He eventually reappeared, red in the face and swearing. He stewed over the unjustified blow to his head until he saw me staring, crooked-faced, through the window. He came over and touched my hand through the glass.

In the late fall, shortly after we'd finished the foundation, 1,981 feet of lodgepole pine logs arrived on a logging truck. It took two loads to deliver the eighty-nine logs, each one twenty to forty feet in length. They came straight from the woods about an hour southwest of the ranch, where a pair of Belgian horses named Sage and Barney skidded them to the road. It was their last job. Their owner, Buck Blakely, retired that year to his cabin in Crescent on the Little Deschutes River. He said that the beavers there were building tremendous dams: "They know what kind of winter looms, and I reckon that by the look of their dams, it'll be beyond the pale of comparison." Dad and I watched him unload the logs as the mountains ate up a storm to the west and its aftermath dissipated over our desert.

I looked to the sky and pleaded for it not to snow anymore.

Dad said flatly, "It won't."

We stood there for a long time after the truck had left. The logs rested in two massive piles, or decks. Each deck was stacked about ten feet high, the logs parallel to each other. They were shaped like a pyramid, wider at the base. Dad had his old drawknife in his hand. He had sharpened it that day for the first time since he built the house I grew up in. He had used it to peel the bark off all the logs for our house and many other houses. He worked for ten years peeling logs at Oregon Log Homes Construction. He was strongest back then, getting paid by the foot.

"Never work with a dull knife," he said and handed it to me.

I took it and noted the weight. He left me there with the logs. I watched him walk back toward the house, not far, but just out of sight. Squinting into the low, bright sun not far off the southern horizon, I sat down, brushing the snow off a log. Letting it bear my weight, I considered what I had taken. Scratching at the log with the corner of the drawknife, the bark came off easily in a big flake. Beneath it I found wild worm lines. They wound around and forked into cul-de-sacs, intricate and beautiful. Usually the drawknife cuts down through the cambium layer of the wood, where the worm lines are. At that moment I decided against the knife, which makes for body-breaking work anyway. I liked the look of the worm lines. Instead, I could slip a chisel or flat piece of metal under the bark and flake it away.

Sitting there in a slouch, I looked out at the giant piles of lodgepole logs that surrounded me. They were a bunch of visitors waiting for me to entertain them. I wondered where they'd come from to make my home. They weren't old-growth redwoods or black-market kona from Hawaii, and they weren't going into a ten-thousand-square-foot weekend home. The logs laid down around me would coalesce into a small, sustainable, human home, but they had been the homes of other creatures first. Forest creatures. When I started to strip them of their bark, tiny seedpods and mushrooms growing on the trunks shriveled as they were exposed to the desert air. For an hour, giant black carpenter ants spilled out the butt of one log, and I watched them race around on the ground, stumbling over each other. But when a tiny, black-and-white-speckled woodpecker that I had never seen in the desert before showed up a few days after the logs, what I had taken sank in. The woodpecker stayed only a little while. Everything else the logs brought died.

The space and machinery needed to manipulate logs is gigantic. I was afraid of the logs, but I trusted my father. Here were the rules—his rules, and now mine, too: never stand too close to the decks, and never to the side, where the logs might roll out and blow out your knee or bust your leg. Never stand on the deck, or it might tumble out from under you. Never roll a log toward yourself. Never walk under a log. On the occasions that you have to get close to it, stand at the end of the deck. Watch for the dog. Keep your fingers and toes out of the way of the logs and the giant steel log tongs that pinch the center of the logs to move them. There needs to be clear communication between the person on the tractor and the person on the ground. Use only very slow, controlled movements once everyone is clear.

"No! Down!" I squawked, frustrated.

"I can't see your fingers with those giant gloves on," Dad bellowed over the tractor. He stood up where he could see my face. "They just look like a ball of leather from here."

"It's fucking cold."

"Hold your hand up! *I. Can't. See. It.*"

I unfurled my fist and stuck my fingers down into the gloves, then pointed to the ground where I needed the log to be. I had to reposition the log tongs. I knew he wanted to drop it hard to the ground, but the log came down slow.

I had received eighty-nine totally random logs, and I needed to look at each of them individually in order to see them together as a house. The log decks needed to be flattened from the stacks they were delivered in. We needed to be able to measure each log—its length, butt, and tip. We needed to see their curvature: Were they crooked and needing to be cut into two short, straight sections? Was there rot?

We moved the logs with our old Farmall tractor. It was old when my grandfather bought it used back in the early seventies. A real champion. The tractor reminded me of a giant red ant with its big back end, five-foot tires, and a seat perched at the rear. To get to the seat, you have to step up on the steel hitches, avoiding delicate hoses and lines. At the helm, gears and levers are at your fingertips, the paint worn off and the metal polished by gloved hands. Half of the gauges work; the others don't matter. The thorax of the tractor holds the engine, totally exposed and fairly easy to work on, all of it covered in black oil and dirt. The exhaust pipe comes right out the top like a train's. The front end has been customized for moving logs, with a stinger extension on the front instead of the bucket. The stinger can telescope as the structure climbs and has log tongs chained to the end, which rig to the approximate center of a log to carry it. The ground was frozen, and Dad sat on the little metal seat of the tractor in his heavy parka. I could barely see his face under his hood, but he was focused on my hands.

I wrangled the logs with my wool hat pulled low and my scarf pulled up over my nose. My eyes watered in the cold, dry wind as I chose the first course of logs. They wanted to tumble and slough out as we pulled pieces from the pile's structure. As soon as we put a little energy to the logs, they would move suddenly, with force, jerking forward and swinging from the tongs. I spent those days cold and scared.

When the weekend rolled around, Mom had some time off work to help me make sense of my logs. We walked up to the decks that Dad and I had laid out and measured.

"Did you read the log-house book?"

"No." The book had been sitting by my bed since I started to dig the foundation three months before. I hate written instructions. I looked at the cover every night before I turned off my light. The picture of an old log cabin motivated me enough to work, but not enough to open the book. "I was hoping you could just explain the basics to me."

"It's complicated."

"Well . . . I know."

She shook her head, again. "You're so experiential, Sarah. You just extrapolate from your available knowledge how to get what you want, and it's often missing 'B' on your way from 'A' to 'C.' That's how you've always been, but this is your house," she said with an emphasis on *house*.

I looked down, a little ashamed.

"You add the logs to the house in courses, or a full layer around the structure." She read the book when she built her house. She chose each log for a particular place. Dad scribed and notched, and then they set each log together, but she was the mastermind. "Each log tapers from its tip to butt, so they are added to the wall in alternating aspects to maintain some semblance of level. If a wall of logs were stacked with the butts to the left and the tips to the right, the wall would be much higher on the left than the right."

I could visualize this, except that my house was shaped like a *T,* not a square. Now I wasn't sure how to make the tip-to-butt thing work.

She tried to draw a picture in the frozen ground with a stick, but it broke. She resorted to a rock. "As the tips and butts come together in a corner from joining walls, they cannot be significantly different in diameter or there will be gaps in the wall for snow, wind, bugs, mice, and flies to get in."

"Right."

"Your logs look good."

We stood at a distance and looked at them. With my brow furrowed and my lips tight, I nodded. There were a lot of logs. Mom sure wasn't overly forthcoming about how to build a house. She never was one to fawn over my projects. I was an arrow and once shot, I was on my own.

"When you set them, put their arc to the outside and slightly up."

I was still nodding to myself when she left. This was complicated, and I should have been reading the book all along. But I wasn't there for some methodical, straightforward process. I was there to wrestle with myself, my dad, logs, concrete, chain saws, whatever. How could a house or a relationship be strong if it wasn't built through struggle and learning and trying so hard that you knew it was for real? I bent my knees and folded onto my side against the hard, bare ground. Chyulu lay down beside me and we looked at the logs from a different angle until we got cold.

THE DESERT AND THE SEA

If my father has a place, it is the sea. Funny that he wasn't born near the water, but rather during the fall of a dry year in Arizona, when the arroyos were parched and the perennial rivers low. He was an army brat, living on posts as placeless and timeless as airports. But when he was in middle school, his father went to Vietnam and his mother, Patricia, moved the family to La Jolla, California. This was when it was still a village, before it became obscenely rich and private. I imagine my father untangling himself from the packed station wagon and sprinting for the saltwater, pulling it to his face. The saltwater seeped into his blood that day, where it still circulates, into the right side of his heart and out the left, to his extremities and back again.

He took up surfing. He rolled down to the breaks in his tiger-striped tank suit after his early-morning paper route and learned how to catch waves. Before long, he moved from the gentle beach breaks, where waves melt into their own faces to Horseshoe and Dunemere reefs. There, the waves are not forgiving. When they hit the reefs they jack up and topple with board-breaking force. No sign of tourists, beachcombers, or surf schools, just steep sandstone cliffs where broken waves crash. Dad paddled out when the swells were the biggest, when their barreling innards held him in dark shadow. He would disappear and then come careening out onto the unbroken face, where he'd pull out over the wave's shoulder as it started to dissipate. They called him Big Wave Dave. They still do.

By the time he was fourteen, he was setting illegal nets off the coast, free-diving fifty feet at night to pull out sixty-pound white sea bass, sharks up to eight feet, and lobster to sell in the neighborhood. He spent his afternoons getting stoned on the beach, looking at the glare off the water with squinted eyes. He went to football practice because his dad, Renn, made him play. His feet were soft from the sea so his cleats gave him blisters. He was small, but buff and dark brown with jet-black hair and an indigenous look to him. A fighter and a free diver. A stoner and a surfer. Not a football player.

By his junior year, he had quit football and started to skip school. My grandfather couldn't understand this seafaring boy with no rural passions or military priorities. One day when David was missing from school, Renn marched to the break to look for him. David was on what he considers the biggest wave he ever caught. He rode it a mile down the beach. Renn said it was the only time he saw his son in action, moving effortlessly with the wild swells on the brink between sea and shore. They never spoke about it, but Renn stopped pestering his son about football.

When David graduated from high school, he thought he could make a life out of the ocean as a merchant marine, so he joined the Maritime Academy. His dad was surprised at the military path, but pleased. David thought he could tolerate a little of the straight and narrow for the possibility of women in every port. But his shaggy hair, VW van, and German shepherd just didn't fit at the academy. He didn't last long.

My grandfather hated the change in La Jolla: the Rolls-Royces, gates, guard dogs, and $20 hamburgers. When he retired as a lieutenant colonel from the army, he wanted land; he preferred a place to raise horses and longhorn cattle. He had grown up on a ranch in Gonzales County, Texas, about eighty miles east of San Antonio. Renn's father had been in the cavalry and had introduced him to horses and long overnight marches. Throughout his military career, Renn's goal was to get back to land that he could work the way he did growing up. He had no ties to the sea, so with David along for the ride after dropping out of the maritime academy, they searched for ranchland from Arizona to Nevada to Oregon while Patricia waited in California. They drank beer for dinner and breakfast until they fell into central Oregon's Lower Bridge Valley. Tucked between two ridges, the 360 acres they found had a well, water rights, and good soil. They called it the LBK, for Renn and his two partners, Blalock and Kibak, who went in on the ranch with him.

They returned to La Jolla just long enough to sell the house on Arenas Street. When they brought Patricia up to the ranch, they swung through Christmas Valley first to show her the place Renn really wanted, a massive spread so far from town that most of the ranchers had airplanes and the women looked more like men. She was appalled, but that was the point. In comparison, the little ranch at Lower Bridge seemed quite civilized. It was within an hour of a town, with good views and other women. Patricia had grown up on a ranch up the Aravaipa Canyon in Arizona, but she'd been to college and Europe and had a career. She wasn't too keen on farmwork, although she did do a lot of irrigating and planted a beautiful garden. She also held on to her sophisticated side by painting, belonging to a book club, and attending church.

Renn was happy to have at least part of his family in one place. But David hadn't planned to stay. He was there just to get the ranch off the ground. His plan was to head south to the land of Latinas, spearfishing, and waves. But one day, when he and Renn were looking to buy longhorns, they saw a woman ride a big sorrel gelding through the auction.

Christine was working for Tom Alexander Quarter Horses at the time, living alone in a trailer, not going to town much except to the bar now and then, when there was music and she could uncork her love for country-western swing. On that day she figured she'd combine an afternoon at the auction yard with an evening of dancing at the 86 Corral. She parked her empty trailer behind the bar and grill, brushed her long, thick brown hair and tucked a fresh pearl-snap Western shirt into her tight, cowboy-cut Wranglers. She didn't bother knocking the mud off her boots. She was a born-again Christian and didn't drink. She was there to swing.

When Christine walked in, Renn recognized her from the auction. She was tall and confident, first with the gelding, and again on the dance floor. He nudged David and pointed her out. David had been drinking tequila and wasn't exactly balanced when he stood up, but he walked over and asked her to dance. He was a poor dancer—bouncy, Mom said—and she was compensating for him. After about ten seconds, he stopped midstride and said, "You're the strongest woman I've ever danced with." As Mom tells it, she knew at that moment she would marry this stranger, this long-haired surfer boy. She told him where she worked and wondered if he would remember through the fog of dance and drink.

To her surprise, David called her the next day and came out to her place for a ride. He'd ridden on a couple of army bases, but unlike any of the other men she'd been with, he was no cowboy. When she mounted him on her boss's retired rope horse, he kicked it into a full gallop down the road and out of sight, much to Christine's horror. She loped after him, thinking how wild and sexy and out of place he was.

Christine was unbelievably steady; she had already traveled abroad and returned to live her dream of breaking horses in central Oregon's ranching country. She had grown up on an apple orchard in the Willamette Valley at a time when she could graze her horse on the median strip of Interstate 5, before it turned into six lanes. She didn't come from a horse family, but when her older sister got pregnant at sixteen, Christine's parents immediately bought her the horse she'd been begging for, because there is nothing like a horse to keep a girl occupied. From then on, she was completely independent, with her own little camp stove and saddlebags. She could take off for days. Eventually Portland swelled and turned the orchard into a retirement community, so she was happy with the central Oregon quiet and the harsh seasons of the high desert that seemed to keep retirees at bay. When she met David, she had her feet on the ground. She wasn't the kind of woman who went to sleep to dream. She was riding young horses the same way David rode big swells, and they fascinated each other.

But David didn't stay long. He had already planned a trip to Costa Rica. He envisioned a life of fresh fruit and surf with a *palapa* on the beach. After he and Christine had dated for a month, he introduced her to his eccentric brother from Los Angeles and headed south. Neither Los Angeles nor the brother was of interest to her. She just kept on going, like David had never wandered into her well-planned life.

Much to his disgust, David's inner ear had calcified closed from the cold, northern Pacific waters. It didn't take long for the tropics to infect his compromised eardrum. Within a few weeks he came home, much short of a lifetime later, in excruciating pain. He was drawn back to Christine like a cold man to a warm fire. Her dutiful care, the desert, and surgery got the ache out of his ear, but it shifted to his soul.

He gave Christine's high desert a chance that turned into a quarter century. In the beginning, she had a job hauling slaughter horses from the Willamette Valley over the Cascade mountains to the Orio Meat Plant in central Oregon, which shipped the meat back to France fresh and hanging. David rode along through the winter, carving antlers and soapstone in the passenger seat. Pulling thirteen horses behind a two-wheel-drive Chevy over the Cascades in winter is a recipe for jackknifes. The first time they blocked the Santiam Pass at Hog Rock, the snowplow driver was annoyed when he had to pull them out. The second time, they could see the headlights of blocked cars winding west all the way out of the mountains. The same snowplow driver looked Christine square in the eyes. "I will not be seeing you here again under *any* circumstances," he said through clenched teeth, then yanked the slack out of the tow chain so hard it knocked the horses down and nearly pulled the front end out of the truck.

They lived in a tiny white house they called the honeymoon cottage. After a couple of years, Christine turned thirty. She decided she needed to get married or move on. David hadn't expected to be confronted like that when it came time to get married, but it made Christine seem even stronger, and he liked that. David's friends made it clear that he was lucky such a mighty woman was willing to marry him. But more than anything, he wanted a family, and that was the only real reason he could think of to get married. Not long after Christine's ultimatum, David found a gold wedding band in the pigpen. He cleaned it up and simply asked Christine if it fit. I imagine them there on a warm day, the doors to the house open, maybe a couple of flies buzzing. Low evening light spills in across the floor. He doesn't look at her at first; he looks at the ring. Then he lifts his dark eyes to meet her steely gray ones, directly level with his own. It fit, and it still does.

My dad hauled a camper back to La Jolla with Mom's Chevy one time before I was born. She was happy to let him go back to the sea. Not only did she love the man she married, she understood him. She expected always to have horses, and she knew he needed the sea. But when he got back to the barreling waves over the La Jolla reefs, someone dropped in on his wave. He tried to pull back as the wave began to pitch, but he was thrown over the falls and pummeled into the flats, blowing out his knee as it came down on his board. For the second time, the sea rejected him, and it was a long time before he tried again.

He returned to central Oregon to farm another man's place while he and Mom saved to buy their own land, which was her dream. Since she was a little girl, she'd wanted a ranch in the high desert with horses, far from town. Dad ran cattle and hayed, moving hundreds of acres of hand line irrigation three times a day, seven days a week. He still talks about that relentless old boss and the hard days he put in before he had a place of his own, which didn't turn out to be any easier. The land strapped him down with bawling cattle, busted equipment, and drought. He would stand out in the field alone and suck in the smoke that was his only peace, keeping his fiery frustration at bay. The stuff that made time stand still, like a portal to his youth on the beach at La Jolla. I wonder if he could feel the world tilt as the moon pulled the ocean, and the ocean pulled him.

RAIN ON SNOW

An old culvert that we pulled up to my site for drainage dumped out a little bit of summer; the dry dirt in it fell onto the vast mud that I'd been wrestling with for weeks. It stopped me and held my attention, a contrast like gold on black. Hard to imagine that they were the same soil. I bent down, took off my wet glove, and put my hand in it.

Dad turned the RPMs down on the tractor and watched. He knew the feeling of longing for something other than mud or frozen ground in winter. Summer and farming felt like so long ago, when the days were warm and long and work was meant to be done. Now the days were short and cold, and every task was a battle. I picked up the dirt and let it fall through my fingers. I blew on it, then threw a handful at Dad. It puffed away and only a couple of grains hit the arm of his jacket.

After Christmas, the weather turned and it started to rain on snow, which made my place a sloppy mess. We couldn't

walk without sinking to our gunnels, let alone move logs
with the tractor. I now had time to peel the bark off every
log in the decks while waiting for the ground to freeze.
Every morning after feeding the horses, I marched up to the
decks and plopped down on a log with a chisel in hand. As I
slid the steel under the loose, moist bark, giant pieces flaked
to the ground.

I could hear my dad in his shop, grinding away on one of
his wood sculptures. He used a chain saw to find the character in the log, roughing out an elephant or a giraffe or a
seahorse or a naked woman. I helped him stabilize a piece of
Mexican ironwood on a platform once and asked him what
it was going to be. He looked at me and said, "I dunno, gotta
look at it first." Eventually the piece comes to him through
his imagination, almost never from a model or a photo. Then
he works on the details with delicate electric tools, grind-
ers and sanders. The finished product is smooth and oiled,
embellishing the color and grain of the wood. I'm sure he
was glad to have a break from the house, the logs, the mud,
the tractor. The struggle of building was like farming, and
he'd had enough. Last summer he told me he was too old to
be as angry as farming made him.

"I'm bound to give myself a heart attack," he said, not
laughing. "It's all I can do not to self-destruct or destruct
whatever is around me."

It made me worry. How many more years of farming did he
have left in him? I planned to take over eventually, but I wasn't
ready yet. I hoped that my presence would make him happy, to
have the next generation willingly in the traces. That he'd be
less lonely. I imagined us farming together and cruising over to

the Oregon coast for a short surf trip if the swell came up. "How can I make this place less maddening for you?" I finally asked.

We were up on the north edge of the property at the hay barn, loading a ton for the horses. "I'm not mad, Sar," he responded, but he looked so agitated with that furrowed brow. It was like something deep down was wrong, but he didn't know what and couldn't really do anything about it. Or at least he wouldn't say.

I pitched up another bale and out of the stack scurried the black barn cat. "I feel sorry for that old barn cat," I said, changing the topic. "No one to feed or love him."

Dad stuck the bale in the stack on the truck and said, "The barn cat is rescued by the nature of its existence. The glory of freedom."

It had always seemed like Dad needed someone to feed and love him, but maybe that wasn't true at all. Or at least it was becoming less true. Somehow related to the barn cat, he said, "I know a guy down on the Saladita point in Michoacán. He's powerful from fishing and surfing every day." Dad flexed his own wiry little body. "He got fifteen hundred hours of surf in last year."

"Wow," I said, still excavating the stack. "How old is he?"

"Forty, maybe." Dad hopped out of the bed of the pickup and set his hay hooks down.

"Does he live with anyone? Is he married?"

"No. He's a surfer," he said, as if to be married and a surfer were mutually exclusive.

Dad pulled the truck out of the barn, and I closed the big wooden doors. Was it possible that a relationship with the sea could actually replace love and intimacy with another human?

Now, sitting with my logs on a cold, wet day, I thought about surfers and barn-cat freedom. Dad wasn't free at all. He had a ranch and a wife and a daughter. He cared for his aging mother and father who lived just a couple hundred yards down the driveway. He helped his sister and brother-in-law farm down the road. He fed all the horses my mom wanted and waited for her return from an office job. He waited out in the dark, exercising. He rode his bike around the compound and lay on one of his long cougar carvings where he paddled with weights. And now he was building a house for his kid. The only thing he did for himself was his sculpture.

So I tried to ask as little as possible of the old man. I sat with my logs and exposed worm lines, finding burls and other elements of character I wanted to show off in my house. The sky pressed in, a low, flat gray, and Chyulu gnawed on a piece of bark. I cut and scraped and pried and thought about how to fight the mud. My time seemed so short and the task too big to cram into a few months. The paralysis that comes with too much to do and not enough time was familiar to me. No matter if I was trying to travel the length of a continent or run the length of a river, I never had enough time.

Glancing up from the bark and my spinning mind, I smiled at my grandma, Mamsy, and her toy poodle, Panchito, puttering toward me. Dressed in heavy canvas and wool myself, I marveled at their ability to persevere on their daily walks despite the mud and cold. "How's the house coming?" she asked as she approached.

"It's not." I felt like everyone I knew was asking me that. Some people even had the nerve to ask if I was living in it. People's minds seemed so skewed in their perception of what it might mean to build a house. This was more than having an idea and hiring a contractor. This was art and the evolution of a structure that had no "plans," and a contractor (me) who had no idea what she was doing.

"You sound a little frustrated."

"Yeah, the mud is really slowing me down." I stuck my leg out, squished my heel into it, and frowned.

"Patience, Sarah. There will always be hurdles, but right now you are staying busy, right? Just remember, this might take longer than you think." She moved on across the rocky ground, knowing I'd bitten off more than I could chew. As she walked away, I wondered if she was thinking about what lessons this house might teach me about patience, which had never been a strong suit of mine.

For two weeks I kept peeling, whacking the idea of patience around in my head like a racquetball. The ball never came to rest, and finally, when I couldn't wait another moment for the ground to cooperate, I took up road construction. I only needed a road about one hundred yards long to get from my log decks to the house site. I was determined.

It was six in the morning, a day in late January, when Mr. Star, the gravel man, buried 53,000 pounds of gravel truck over its axles in the mud morass. He called me the morning the temperature had dropped enough to freeze the ground, so he could deliver the rock at dawn before the ground thawed. I heard him coming from the gap at Lafollette Butte, two miles away. I opened the wire gate, and he gave me a wave as he kept his momentum. I ran after him toward my house site, cutting across the rocks and through the barbed-wire fence just as he turned around to back into position so he could get a good spread pulling out. I expected him to stop and check the ground. In spite of the cold, I had buried my truck there the day before, moving rocks into the mud ruts in the dark. He gunned the dump truck in reverse for momentum and sank it there at the base of the hill. I stood about fifty yards away, out of breath. I wasn't in a hurry any-more and closed the distance at a walk, gathering myself.

Dad and I tried to fire up the big International tractor to pull the gravel truck out, but it didn't have glow plugs for heating the air in the engine cylinders and hadn't been started since summer. We hooked the tractor up to the truck with cables for a half hour, a heater on the oil pan. Mr. Star seemed patient enough. He waited in the distance, talking on his cell phone. When we tried again to start it, there was still way too much cold engine to turn over on that subzero morning. I ran up and called one of my neighbors. Russell was just walking out the door to feed his cattle. He fired up his big new tractor instead and came straight over. After Mr. Star dumped the gravel in one giant pile, Russell yanked that fat purple truck out of the slurry and sent the man on his way.

I hadn't talked to Russell before that winter. I knew his truck, and his pretty wife and adopted kids, but as far as I knew, he just circled his fields opposite ours. I had always been too young to know him personally. He moved fast, and I never had a need real enough to stop him. After he helped with the gravel truck, I dropped off a case of Dr. Pepper for him, his favorite soda. Later that winter he dragged my truck out of a snow drift, and we commiserated about the weather, talking like neighbors for the first time.

It took more than a week for the ground to freeze hard enough for Mr. Star to deliver the rest of the rock: six truckloads of three-inch rock. The road had to cover only the 250 feet from the log decks to the house, but the mud swallowed up all that rock. Mr. Star was able to spread a couple of loads, but had to dump the others after the first load blocked the way—piles of rocks frozen in place. The piles seemed like mountains. The fact that they were frozen slowed me down for days. I couldn't shovel or rake frozen rock, so I gathered it in five-gallon buckets by hand and sprinkled it systematically in layers over the mud, my Dad working contentedly in his shop all the while.

When I tired of building the road by hand, I could haul hay on the frozen ground. Dad had another hay customer who wanted eighty tons hauled for his cows. There were others, too, ladies with a couple of horses that needed a couple of tons of hay, a horse barn that went through a ton every three days, plus our own forty horses, who ate three tons a week. Generally, I hauled hay in the morning when the ground was hard, then spread buckets of gravel in the afternoon when it warmed up. But with road construction at an icy creep, I hauled a lot of hay.

One evening when I went down to the hay barn for my fourth load, the wind picked up and boomed out of the south. The walls of the hay barn trembled, and sheet metal snapped against itself. I found a calm eddy inside the east wing and let my tired body down onto the tailgate of the truck to look out into the sky. A swath of dark crystal blue set against the black of everything beneath it. A raven, suspended in the unobstructed current beyond the barn, cocked its wings perfectly to let the wind pass above and below its body. Suddenly, with the slightest change of its wing, a current caught it in the chest and flicked the bird into the night.

I had wasted the last moments of dusk watching the raven, so I loaded the hay in the dark by memory and drove home against the wind. I listened to it blow past the crack in the window. The gravel road made the old door squeak. I twirled my dog's hair around my finger and drove slow.

Two weeks after the delivery of the first load of gravel, the tractor climbed blissfully over the mud bog, a foot of rocks between it and us. No matter how miraculous it seemed to build a house, the road was my biggest accomplishment of the winter. Dad came trundling down the road to the log decks, where they were laid out over about two acres, sorted by length and diameter. He pulled up perpendicular to the center of the first log with the tractor and lowered the log tongs. The tractor idled in front of the thirty-six-foot log for the base of the north wall. I don't know what made us think we should move the biggest log in the deck for our trial run. I hammered the tongs into the log and Dad picked it up. The goal was to get the tongs just slightly off center so the log would be lighter on one end. If the tongs were perfectly centered, the log teeter-tottered and that made it hard to control. If the tongs were slightly to one side, I could hold the lighter end down with my body and help guide it the hundred yards to the house from the log decks.

Dad waited for me to get clear. I called Chyulu and told him to stay under a tree. The rhythm of the tractor engine was muffled through my earplugs. With eye contact, he pressed the lever down, and the hydraulics labored to lift the log. I hung on the light end to keep the log counter-balanced, but once we got under way it was so enormous that it dragged me across the ground even with my heels dug in. I was completely out of control and scared, but we guided it through trees and bitterbrush, past the gate and around to the back of the house. Pulling with all my might, I got the log parallel to the side of the tractor to fit through tight spots. I couldn't hold the log back, but I could pull against the momentum of the tractor to get the other end of the log through the trees and then swing forward to miss the gate. It had to be a fluid movement, using the momentum of the log against the movement of the tractor, which was difficult to coordinate between me on the ground and Dad on the tractor.

Suddenly, the log caught on a tree, pulling far back along the right side of the tractor and lifting me off the ground. I let go and ran to get out of the way. As Dad pulled forward, the log snapped loose from the tree and swung like a baseball bat, crashing into the side of the foundation.

"Didn't you know that was going to happen? Why'd you pull forward?" I yelled when the dust had settled.

"What? Did you think you were going to hold that giant log back? What else could we have done to fit this thing back here around the trees that you wouldn't pull out to make room for this kind of construction?"

"I like the trees." I glared at him, irritated by the blame.

Dad turned off the tractor. "We need to take a break."

"Shouldn't we set it?" This was the first log, and we'd come so far. I wanted to see it on the foundation so badly.

"No. Time for lunch. I can't deal with this kind of shit on an empty stomach."

I stood there by the dinged corner of my foundation and looked at the log on the ground. I took my earplugs out and put them in my pocket. They were black with engine oil and earwax. Dad grabbed his little blue bag with a half-eaten apple and piece of toast that he ate one bite at a time, iced tea in his tippy-cup and his medicine bottle of weed. He headed home with Chyulu nosing around in the satchel by his side for a tennis ball. I ran after them.

"Thanks, Dad, this is exciting!" I felt like I could lose him any minute. That he would tire of the project and me. It was a lot to ask of him after a long summer of farming.

"It's been ten years since I built my house, and this is all too familiar."

"Well, at least we get to be together."

"Yeah, Sar, it's good to be together." He patted me on the shoulder. "Maybe you could help me haul some hay for the horses after we finish working this afternoon."

"Sure." I was definitely indebted to him for all of his help, and if I didn't keep him happy, he wouldn't continue helping and the whole project would grind to a standstill. Both the house and our relationship.

After setting that giant log, which took all afternoon, Dad drove me down to the hay barn at dusk to fetch some bales for the horses. His hip was bothering him, so he left me in the nearly dark barn while he wandered around the west wall to take a hit and check out the sunset. I grabbed a stack of bales with my hay hook and pulled them down to load, careful of my footing in the dark.

"Seer!" That's what he called me when he was feeling friendly or playful. He said it with a little squeak. "You gotta come check this out right now. I reckon it's the most beautiful sunset I've ever seen."

I stepped out of the truck bed nice and slow, easing around a mess of hay bales.

"Hurry it up. It's gonna change, and I know you're gonna fight me on it for fifty years, but this is purt'near the prettiest one of my life."

I stepped out a little faster, and he opened his arm to throw over my shoulder. We turned our faces into the orange light and he laughed, "Look at those colors! That salmon on turquoise. It looks like a swell, picked right up out of the ocean. Maybe I could ride it on my blue board." He swept his hand across the sky. "Shwoosh," he said, and laughed hard with an open mouth. Dad had been riding the same baby blue longboard since he was a teenager in La Jolla. It was a nine-foot, six-inch beast with a redwood stringer, and it called to him. Together, they needed the sea. "Can't you just see us out there? I tell ya, you haven't been laughing until you cry, but those colors up there are coming at me in misty ribbons. Beautiful." Then silence as the sunset waned.

I turned to him, the light now purple on his toothy grin and in his watery eyes. I remember thinking how adorable he was all dressed in greasy canvas, with the hat I had knit for him pulled down to his tweaky eyebrows. Underneath all that was his tan little body, fit from paddling every night with weights on a log in the dark. He was fixated on being ready when it was time to head back to the sea with the blue board.

I walked back to the truck and loaded it by feel in the pitch black. He wandered over with his hands in his pockets. "When you're here by yourself, don't forget to take the time to watch the sunset." His voice trailed out of the dark.

I stopped for a minute. What did he mean, by myself? I didn't know what to say so I said, "Okay."

THE HANGMAN BRAND

My parents were married in October, on one of those perfect days when the wind stops blowing the warmth of the sun away. My mom, cool in a plain Gunny Sack dress; Dad, hot in a blue suit, his hair long and black. Mom had let him pick out the cake, which was not white, but bright orange with brown flowers. In the pictures, everyone's mouths were dyed orange. In the shade of an old juniper on the ranch, they looked happy, or maybe just laughing at each other's carroty lips. That night Dad got as drunk as Mom had ever seen him, and she poured him into bed. I wonder if all that tequila was in celebration of a new life, or if Dad was drowning the pain of his divorce from the ocean. I wonder if he knew how many years could slip away on a ranch in the desert.

Shortly after the wedding my parents bought some Texas longhorns, and they needed a brand. I imagine them sitting at the kitchen table in the honeymoon cottage, surrounded by their recently discovered and refinished hardwood floor. The brown shag carpet probably still sat in a heap out back. Dad scribbles on scraps of paper. They now share the same last name. Lawrence. *L*. I imagine them turning the letter upside down and sideways, adding dots and bars. They must have written from every angle of the paper, turning and checking. Somehow they digressed into a game of hangman. I can't even imagine what the word might have been, but the hangman brand came out of it. They laughed at the thought of this land-and-livestock dream hanging them in the end. The gallows and a dangling head would mark their place and herd as their ranch grew slowly over the next twenty years.

One of my only memories of the longhorns was of terror. I was maybe four years old, stuck in the old red Chevy while my parents tried to corral a raging bull. I crouched on the floorboard and held my breath as the bull slammed repeatedly into the side of the truck. My parents hollered outside, but I could not see them. I braced my arms against the dashboard and seat to keep from being thrown around when the truck got knocked one way or the other. The bull was young, but approaching breeding age, and we had to get him out of the pasture he shared with his mother.

When the thrashing subsided for a moment, I sat up on the bench seat and looked between the gun racks out the back window. Geraldine's son, Devereau Cavanaugh, was climbing out of his big black truck. Dev was born about a hundred years too late. He leaned on the front of his truck, in his cowboy boots, tight Wranglers, black wool jacket, and silk scarf. With his thick black mustache and a black felt hat pulled low, he looked like he should have been robbing trains or killing Indians. He took stock of the situation, then unloaded his big roping gelding out of his trailer, eased into the saddle, and loped off in the direction of the longhorn herd where the young bull was making mischief.

My mom gave me a reassuring smile, but held her post at the back door of the trailer. The plan was to rope the bull and then drive or drag him into the trailer. We didn't have corrals that would make this task easier. Instead, we were trying to drive a bull into the back of a trailer that sat out in the open on a hundred acres. Some might argue that this is impossible. Eventually, Dev got a rope around the bull's horns, which turned out to be a bad idea. Because he was mounted, he had to stay behind the bull, and the result was a mix of driving the beast and being dragged by it.

Fifty feet from the trailer, the bull dodged left and dragged Dev and his horse into the half-frozen irrigation pond, all of them swimming and breaking ice as they went. They climbed out soaking wet, and again Dev drove the bull toward the open door of the trailer. I crouched in the truck and peeked out at the mayhem. The bull ran straight at the back of the trailer, then split to the left, spun around, and rammed the truck. I dropped back to the floorboard and held on.

Dev eventually lost hold of the rope and the bull took off with it, back to his herd. Dev loaded his wet horse in his trailer and left, pissed. My parents resolved to build a corral, and we went home.

When we showed up a few days later with the corral built, the rope wasn't on the bull anymore. It was around his mother's horns, and she had wound it around a telephone pole till her face was held flat against the pole. Her name was Blondie. She was my favorite cow. She was big and aggressive and beautiful. My mom cut the bull out of the herd with her quick bay mare. She pushed him toward the corral with the cushion of respect that moves cattle. She didn't need to be close; she just needed to be in the corner of the bull's eye wherever he turned, to move him the other way. The bull ran into the corral, took one look at the high pole fence, reared up, and set his body down over the poles. They snapped and blew out of their posts, and he walked out. Dad stood there, flabbergasted.

Getting that bull out of the herd turned out to be impossible, and it wasn't worth the trouble to let him keep his testicles. Not long after that, the vet came out to tranquilize the bull. He loaded the dart gun with enough drugs to nearly kill him, but the drug didn't even slow him down. The vet had to dart him twice before he crumpled to the ground from a dead run. We castrated him there in the sand and left him in the herd.

Dad grew tired of the longhorns and the way they tied him down with feeding and fixing fences. Raised as a mover, Dad fell into our place like someone might fall into a hole—with a jolt on a locked knee. His mind strained against the cold barbed wire that he stretched on flat gray winter days after the cattle busted the fence. He couldn't help thinking about what he could have had if he hadn't gotten that ear infection in Costa Rica. I can imagine him mindlessly bending and twisting the barbed wire with his leather-clad hand, dreaming of surf, Latina women, and weed. In an effort to forget the first two, he turned to the latter, which got him thrown in jail.

He did his time, and I wonder if in jail there was a little

sense of relief from the ranch. Back in those days, growing for personal use would get you put away for a month. When he got out, Mom threatened to leave him if he didn't give up the marijuana. But he wouldn't do it. He got back to the ranch and all those cattle with the gallows branded on their asses, and he couldn't get through a single day without getting high. To Dad, the ranch was Mom's dream, and he was doing the best he could. It wasn't a bad dream. They still had each other, but it wasn't his dream. I suppose Mom thought at one point that he would grow up and quit. Or that she could love it out of him. She realized she couldn't and that their life together couldn't be bigger than the drug. When I asked her once why she never left him, she said she accepted two things: him and her inability to change him.

My mom has an incredible ability to forgive and move forward. It comes from deep inside her, not from reasoning or because Jesus says it's the right thing to do. It comes without suppressing what could easily be resentment. She can't help herself. Plus, she loved my dad. He was a good man, a smart man, a sidesplittingly hilarious man, and he was different from all the conservative rednecks around. He was almost exotic. But as fun as it is to have something exotic, the exotic tends to perish, lose its mind or its feathers or its hair; eventually it gets a disease, escapes, or dies. Mom loved the guy, despite the fact that maybe she should have let him go, back to the sun and the sea. If she could deal with what it took for him to live out there in the desert, the surfer rancher would survive, and she had faith that they would have a good life together.

So weed became a permanent part of our lives, with no more hopes that it might go away. Every morning Dad stood with his right foot on the floorboard of his old red Chevy and bellowed, "I'm comin'," to the Texas longhorns and forty horses bawling and nickering from the dry ground. They had a well-worn path where the fence line dipped past his bedroom window. He could not sleep in. He kept his one-hitter and his medicine bottle of Mexican bud in his left coat pocket, where Mom chose not to dig. He held that blue smoke deep as he slid across the bench seat of the truck, where the red vinyl was gone and the yellow sponge cushion disintegrated.

Dad flew under the radar out in the desert, where he could work without a criminal check. He farmed and ranched and dealt with it the only way he knew how: smoke. But guilt and paranoia turned over in his stomach. He blamed his constant indigestion on a dairy allergy. Different, lawless, and constantly fighting the lazy mind-suck of pot, he became a paranoid workaholic. The neighbors knew his story, and when a ranch sold in the valley, it came with gossip. Even though our neighbors generally fell into the category of "rural conservative," no one ever said anything to Dad's face. Still, he knew they knew, and it isolated him. On top of that, he knew his wife didn't like the smoke and that ate away at him.

I personally didn't find out about my dad and weed until I was a senior in high school. When I was headed to New Zealand to study abroad, Dad pulled his pictures out to show me the waves from his several months there surfing during his twenties. He had all kinds of advice about where to get a surfboard, and he checked three times that I had packed my wetsuit. In the moments when the thought of a full year away scared me and I almost decided to stay home, Dad got out his pictures again and told me how excited he would be to visit me down there.

Dad had taught me to surf when I was eight. I remember him standing out in the surf with me, sending me down tiny wave faces on my tummy. I loved the cold, bubbly saltwater on the Oregon coast and the ritual with my dad on our rare vacations at the beach, because a ranch is a hard thing to leave. Dad calls it his ball and chain. We would wake up early and drive to the point at Seaside to check the surf. Mom would stay at the beach house to fix breakfast and work on some five-thousand-piece puzzle. I held the binoculars on my lap. The hay and dust crusted in the seams of the truck became suddenly pungent when we drove into the coastal humidity. Dad would park where we could see the surf from inside the truck. I let him look through the binoculars, which he spent a long time doing, while I waited for the verdict.

How big were the waves? Where was the swell coming from? How was the wind blowing? We hoped for a southern swell that would wrap around the point for a clean break, with a light offshore wind to stand the waves up nicely, but our beach outings were rare, so we usually paddled out no matter what. Surfing for me meant cold wetsuits and ice-cream headaches when the waves crashed over my head. It meant struggling to paddle out through the waves and, just before making it far enough, getting pummeled by a big set that knocked me off my board and sent me back to start over. It meant saltwater so deep in my sinuses that it would spontaneously release when I had my head over my dinner plate, filling the plate with saltwater and soaking my food. But it also meant witnessing my father in his element. He could make it out through the waves without even getting his hair wet, and then he'd catch the biggest wave of the set and come sailing in to cheer me on. His style was classic and smooth, and I recognized him by his slicked-back silver hair and his arched stance with hands up, like the first stage of prostration. I paddled harder when he was watching me. Other surfers noticed him on the biggest waves with his old blue board, and they'd ask him about places he had surfed and where he got his classic board, why he wore Wranglers, cowboy boots, and a flannel shirt. I always wanted to be like him, but I was just his dorky sidekick.

When I arrived in New Zealand, I immediately made friends with some boys who surfed and bought myself a bright yellow longboard. I took the bus to the beach after school and paddled out no matter how small the waves were. The water was warm enough to surf without a wetsuit, which I found glorious. After a few months, I felt confident on the waves. Surfing wasn't such a battle anymore, but every day that I paddled out, I missed my dad. It wasn't the same without him. I realized I surfed for him. I interacted with the sea for him, and I couldn't wait for him to come down to see me at my own surf break with my own surfboard and my own friends. I was living the way I'd imagined he had as a young man in La Jolla, and I knew he'd be proud. But when he and Mom landed in New Zealand, the airport authorities brought out the drug-sniffing dogs. They found an ounce of weed in Dad's underwear. Mom stood in the customs line alone, pissed beyond tears, while Dad got deported. She had accepted his habit, but what idiot would carry marijuana through New Zealand customs? The country is an island, and they make you clean the mud off your shoes before entering. Not to mention the fact that they grow some of the best weed in the world.

Mom and I had a good vacation, but I didn't surf. It didn't matter anymore. I had never traveled alone with her before. We had always been on a surf trip with Dad. This time we perused county fairs and craft markets and hiked wilderness trails. We lay restlessly beside each other in funky motels talking about Dad and weed. I felt like an adult, and he seemed like a child. It was the beginning of a role reversal: Mom kept her place while Dad and I switched. He went back to the ranch and the hangman brand, where he lied and told his parents he had developed another ear infection and had to come home. When my year was up and I had to go home, I was afraid to accept my dad as a stoner. I was sure that this new knowledge would somehow change everything about him.

When I pulled up the driveway a few days before Christmas, my senior year of high school, Dad walked out of his shop wearing layers of winter canvas. I walked to him and took him in my arms, then squeezed until I could feel his little body deep inside all those clothes. In the days that followed, I realized that he was the same dad I always knew. A little quirky, with wild ideas about how to make a buck. He worked just as hard all week, rode horses with me after school, and skied with me on the weekends. He still had the same lyrical, kind of poetic, way of speaking. We played basketball on the sloping dirt driveway with the fifteen-foot basket that didn't have a net. He still felt hanged by the cold and the cattle, but despite occasional explosions of cussing and spitting and losing his mind, he kept his sense of humor.

He'd have my mom and me in stitches laughing every night, at the absurdity of him, of all people, living this strange life here. He told the kind of anecdotal stories from his days on the farm that you really only laugh at after the fact, but he laughed, and we laughed with him. He still talked about waves at the dinner table. And I talked about rivers. And Mom looked out the window. I decided to ignore the weed, so I never asked him about it, and for a long time it went away.

LEARNING TO FARM

Most of what our family knows about farming in the Lower Bridge Valley my mom learned from a man named Don Williams. Don had lived in the valley and knew the weather and where it came from. Clouds roll over the mountains from the west, but the rain really comes from the south in the summer. Giant thunderheads build beyond the flat horizon, out where the planet bends away. They rise white, tight and tall with black bottoms, and sweep over the fresh-cut hay, turning it into worthless tobacco. Sometimes they'll bring dime-size hail and torrents to the gully past the house. Don and Mom often stopped on Lower Bridge Road and idled side by side until their trucks were nearly out of gas. Mom loved Don and the sense of belonging he gave her. She relayed everything to Dad, and with that, they learned to farm.

By the time we moved to the valley, Don's son, Tom, had taken over his operation. It didn't matter how long and hot the days were, what broke down, what got rained on; he loved to farm. Mom always hoped Tom's enthusiasm would rub off on my dad, who approached farming more like war. Ironically, it was Tom who lost the battle.

One summer day a storm welled in the south, headed for Tom's bales. Maybe he didn't set the safety on the hydraulic bed of the bale wagon. Maybe it failed. It was the last load of the day. Don had gone back to the house. When Tom didn't come back, Don eventually went back down to the field. He found the bale wagon idling by the stacks, but Tom didn't respond when he yelled. I don't know if the metal bed wasn't sitting right, as if something, or someone, was blocking it. Maybe there was blood pooled under the machine. I imagine Don rushing on his old legs to the controls in the cab, slapping the hydraulic lever down, and waiting by the side of the machine while the bed slowly raised, exposing his son's crushed body.

Don hurried to the house to call. But he didn't call the ambulance. He called my godmother, Gudrun, because he knew she had been a nurse in World War II. She called the ambulance before she ran out the door and sped to the field. Gudrun was a stoic Dane. She had moved up from La Jolla with my grandmother and embraced the rural life with fervor. I can't imagine what she found in the field that day, but for hours, she was all there was. The ambulance got lost and couldn't find them. No one could have revived Tom, but I can't imagine the helplessness she must have felt.

My dad was a pallbearer at Tom's funeral. Tom had counted my parents among his best friends. On the surface, they didn't seem close. They talked, mostly about farming, and the weather, of course. But it was more than that. Farming was a community event. There was comfort in seeing another man circling the ground in the distance. Our lives were transparent. We knew everything about our neighbors without having to talk to them. We knew when their hay got rained on or their equipment broke down. We knew they'd had a good year when they were driving a new car. We saw them working, and it gave us extra endurance. We knew if they'd been attentive to their irrigation or if they'd left streaks of dry ground and brown grass. We knew if they'd staked their wheel line at the end of summer or left it to turn into a pretzel in the fall winds. We knew if they survived one of the toughest jobs—or if they had rushed.

After Tom died, tears would well up and run down Don's face every time Mom saw him. People imagine farmers and ranchers to be stoic, silent, but Mom always said that the isolated men of the land were the most in touch with their feelings and not afraid to show them on the rare occasion that someone was listening. Tom had farmed hundreds of acres before he died, and Don didn't have anyone to take over the operation. Some of those acres were leased from Priday and Catherine Holmes. One of the leased pieces was a twenty-five-acre field that sat at the corner of Lower Bridge and Holmes roads. It was part of an eighty-acre parcel adjacent to my grandparents' place. Don offered to turn over the lease to my mom, because he knew my parents were looking for some land of their own.

Priday and Catherine Holmes had bought the eighty acres for tax reasons in the 1930s. They hoped that one of their kids would eventually want it, but were happy to turn the lease over to my parents. There's nothing like seeing a young couple learn to farm through all the struggles and tiny triumphs. Each year, my mom and I would go over to make our lease payment and have cookies. Their house was full of memorabilia from their ranching days. An early aerial photo of the ranch hung on the wall, and Mom and I marveled that the place was bare, compared to the juniper forest today. The Holmeses had been farming or grazing every square inch.

Each year, Mom asked if they would sell us the place. Around the third year they must have figured my parents had earned the right to own the land. Maybe they had lost hope of getting their own kids to farm it. So they started to dicker over a price. When Mom checked back with Priday, he would say that he was talking to people. One man told him the place was worth about $100,000. That made Mom's heart sink. Buying land when you were young and broke was a thing of the past. A person had to inherit it, especially if they had gotten all tied up in longhorn cattle. But Priday said they were still doing some figuring. My parents were doing some figuring of their own and decided that they could afford to pay $40,000 if the Holmeses would carry the contract. When Mom called again, Priday had decided on a price.

"I'd like to sell the eighty acres for $32,100."

Mom stood silent on the other end of the phone, there by the kitchen window in the old yellow farmhouse that we rented. I was playing on the floor.

"Are you there, Christine?"

"Yes. Yes, I'm here," she said. "We can do that!" I can imagine her heart racing and her mind's eye scanning the ground that would be ours, the long parcel laid out in front of her from the high rimrock, deeded irrigation water flowing down the north side through two ponds to the field. A rare patch of ground in that shallow dirt country, it had deep, dark, loamy soil. It was real land. And it would be in our name. That must have been one of the best days of my parents' lives, as they danced and squealed under the old poplar trees in the sun. Even my dad was excited. At least he could work his own place instead of someone else's. It may have been Mom's dream to live on the farm in central Oregon with horses and cattle, building her own house and life there—she was a real back-to-the-lander. But now Dad shared the dream, too. She had given him a family that he lived for, and together they were about to do something that neither of them could do alone.

Not long after we bought our land, Don sold his place and moved to town. He was ancient by then. New farmers in the valley began to ask my parents for advice. And they shared what they knew as Don had done all those years before. We depend on the knowledge of the people who go before us, before we become our own experts. It was the way we tried to evolve without repeating our mistakes. The way history and knowledge moved was what intertwined our lives, through the land and into each other.

MEN IN WINTER

As winter wore on, the house progressed from a fetal position to a kneel, and then the weather got harsher. Winds desiccated what had for weeks been saturated ground. Snow blew away, except where it caught in the eddies behind trees and the leeward sides of irrigation lines. Mixed with dust, it looked like the white sands of the Gobi. It was a Thursday, and by the time Dad and I arrived at the house, after all the chores were done, the day was practically over. I pulled the saw out of the back of the truck, and it fell heavy against my thigh. Dad adjusted his safety glasses.

"I should be in Mexico . . . or Bali, maybe," he grumbled.

I didn't look at him or respond. I just worried to myself that I might lose him at any moment, that he'd explode and hate me for dragging him through this ludicrous project at the worst time of year. I wiped my cold nose on my sleeve, rolled my earplugs between my fingers, and pushed them in deep before choking my saw. Before pulling the cord, I glanced at Dad, who was bobbing his head, along with his internal dialogue.

Ten big pulls on the cold saw and I stood, rubbing my shoulder. I tried again and adjusted the choke. Not a chance in that cold. Standing over my saw, I considered for a moment what was important for that day. That house had been driving us both hard.

I lugged the saw back to the truck and set it on the tailgate. "Let's go, before either of us gets frustrated beyond recovery," I said calmly, with a twinge of defeat.

He didn't object, so we bumped home across the horse pasture to do something else for the day. Anything else.

"I'm seriously thinking about heading south for some waves," he said before he stepped out of the truck to open the wire gate.

It had been a long time since he'd gone anywhere for waves. He'd resigned himself to the ranch and the life he'd chosen, and he'd rather not go without his wife, who worked a normal job with only two weeks' vacation.

"Maybe we could take a trip to the Oregon coast," I said when he got back in the truck. "It's been a while since we took a surf trip over there. We used to go twice a year."

"Yeah, I remember. We could try," he said. He looked a bit relieved at just the thought of the beach.

I left Dad in his wood shop, out of the wind. I headed to the wood pile to try to do something with my day. After splitting a cord of wood, I walked in the door to stoke the stove and the phone rang. It was a desperate cowboy. He was down to a rotten bale and a few flakes and wanted three tons. Hauling hay was the kind of activity that could possibly fend off frostbite, so I hooked up the flatbed trailer and headed to the hay barn. My cheeks and ears ached the second I stepped out of the truck, as my blood pushed into them.

I moved fast, kneeing and yanking and bucking bales across the flatbed. I laid the first layer down and started the second. Carrying a bale at my waist, I danced across the first layer, careful not to fall between the bales, pitching them up to make the third row, then the fourth, then the fifth. At that point in the winter, it took me about fifteen minutes a ton, or thirty seconds a bale. I jumped down, grabbed my straps out of the truck bed, and slung them over the load. Running around to the other side, I tied my knots, fumbling the rope with my heavy gloves, then sprinted to the door, jumped in, and threw the key over. Jabbing the heater button, I slid the temperature to full red and buckled over in my seat, gasping for warmer air, rubbing my aching hands on my thighs as the blood ventured into them again. I cried out at the pain, over the blasting heater, rocking myself alone there in the truck.

The sky looked like the palm of an icy hand, open, pressing down. I could feel its weight. With my forehead pressed against the steering wheel I wondered what the hell I was doing there, back in central Oregon, instead of lounging around on a river in some South American summer. I never said anything of the sort to my father, who wondered the same thing aloud every day. I didn't want to admit that I struggled with the cold too—that dreams of water and endless summer lingered from my travels despite my resolution to move back to the ranch. On days like this, I questioned my certainty about where I belonged. Seeing my dad struggle made me wonder even more. Lifting my head, I squinted into the steely distance and fought to replace those thoughts with the goal of taking over the farm, believing I could do it better than Dad—that I could be happier. Believing that this land, in any season, was home and where I was meant to be.

Eventually my body stopped burning, and I pressed in the clutch and rolled out of the barnyard in low gear. The cold was manifest in everything. The washboard on the gravel road felt like it would bounce my rig to pieces. Tires flicked gravel over the frozen ground and sculpted the road into sharp, rock-hard ridges.

As I passed my neighbor Travis's place on the way out, the rear right tire on the trailer blew out. Somehow, I wasn't surprised. Doing anything in that weather was like picking a fight. I jogged past my neighbor's elk herd to the house, where I found the ladies and kids playing their fiddles and guitars. When I opened the door, a blast of wood-fire heat hit my face. The warmth was laced with the sweet smell of fresh bread. I stepped in and started to overheat. The ladies invited me to stay, but I couldn't stand the idea of peeling off my wraps and putting them back on.

I wandered through myriad barns—a hay barn, a semi-truck barn, a tractor barn, a tool barn, a junk barn, a horse barn—until I finally found Travis in the woodshed. He acknowledged me with eye contact and a possible grunt from under his scarf.

"Sorry to bother you, but I've got a flat tire on my trailer and it's loaded," I said sort of sheepishly. "Do you think you could help me out?"

"Is it that old, hand-built flatbed trailer?" he asked.

"That's the one."

"I reckon I might have a spare that would work," he said and dropped his ax, pulling down his scarf. "How's the cold treatin' ya?" he asked as we gathered up a block and the tire and drove to the road.

"Oh, fine," I lied, putting up a half-hearted, tough attitude.

Travis stood a good foot taller than me, and his layers seemed heavier than mine. He had the look of a classic, old-time cowboy. When I saw him at gatherings he wore a vest and Western shirt, pressed jeans and cowboy boots. Today he wore insulated overalls, a thick wool jacket, and his black cowboy hat, even though it left his ears exposed. Committed to the look, I thought. Why not a wool hat? Who needs a full brim on a flat gray day? But I wasn't about to ask him. His long cinnamon beard caught ice crystals on his chest. He didn't usually say much, but on that day he said a lot. He told me stories of growing up when it was forty below most days; he made it sound like winter engulfed ten months of the year. I don't know if that made me feel better about the winter and my life or not. We changed the tire, and he sent me on my way.

Creeping down the road in my two-wheel-drive truck, I realized I hadn't ever had a conversation with Travis before. At a mile away, he was my closest neighbor, and not once had we had an interaction until now. And he immediately felt like a friend, someone who shared this country and its hardships. We talked freely, and I felt as if layers of history and community were peeling away. I had spent my whole life in this valley and people knew who I was, much to my surprise. I belonged. My dad never felt any sort of community here. He didn't talk to the neighbors. He didn't ask for help or borrow equipment. He marveled at the assistance I was able to conjure up. Russell had never been to our house before, and there he was with his tractor. Travis was enormous and silent, and here we were laughing on the side of the road, frozen to the bone. Then I drove away with a tire that he'd just given to me. I might have been missing out on the culture and community and language in Chile, but my dad was missing out on the same thing in his own home.

I unloaded hay in the dark for the desperate cowboy and drove home in a blizzard at ten miles per hour. The radio didn't work, so I leaned forward in the quiet with my eyes fixed on the road, wondering if I did the work for the money or the good karma. When I pulled into the driveway, the house was dark, my parents gone to bed. I climbed up the stairs without dinner and lay in bed, too tired to eat, listening to my window flex in the storm. In the split second before falling asleep, I felt grateful that this had been the first day cold enough to keep me from building. Despite all the mud and snow and every other damn thing, I realized I had persevered no matter how slow it felt. It gave me a tremendous sense of earning.

In the morning, I wandered downstairs and shuffled to the north window to check the temperature. Slightly warmer. Ten below. I buttered toast and served eggs while Mom finished cutting an orange. We ate and talked about the tractor, which had been giving us fits when we needed it to move logs. The glow plugs on the tractor were not doing their job of preheating the cylinders.

"The button for the glow plugs hangs out from under the steering wheel now," I said with a mouthful of toast. "It dangles by some frayed wires."

I had to take off my gloves and use both hands in a fist to squeeze the button. It felt strange to have my hand complete an electrical connection. I wondered every day if I might get electrocuted, but Dad didn't seem too worried. For the past week it had been nearly impossible to complete the connection. Dad and I would each squeeze and readjust until our hands were frozen or exhausted, then trade out. The process had become asinine.

"We can't move logs without that tractor," I said, searching for some sense of how to deal with it.

As she did for all of our problems, Mom had a solution. "Well, if you can get the part out and get the number off it, you could get it in town," she said with a snicker. She knew Dad and I were wholly unwilling to drive to town. We'd jury-rig anything before driving to town. It took only about forty-five minutes to get there, but it was a completely different world of traffic and new roads, including a new four-lane highway. All the small equipment or ranch supply stores were impossible to get in and out of.

"Town?!" We exclaimed in unison.

"Aren't you going to town today?" I asked her.

Mom always found our disdain for the drive amusing, since she did it every day. "Yeah, I can pick it up for you," she said and shook her head.

"Thanks, Mom!" I said. I felt a new impetus to solve the problem and headed out to dismantle the tractor. I had been overwhelmed with having to work on the tractor before I could get to the construction. As if the building wasn't demanding enough.

Dad and I endured a long, bitter morning crammed together in the side of the tractor—a tight spot with no leverage, systematically stripping the bolt with our open-ended wrench. We clearly needed a box wrench with a cheater that could extend its handle and increase our leverage in order to get the glow plug button out of the old Farmall. We unwedged our thickly clad shoulders from the side of the tractor and stood back, disgusted.

"Damn it!" I yelled and turned away.

"Never yell at anything from closer than thirty feet, Sarah—when you're this close you need to whisper, or it might explode on you." He was only half joking, but we laughed, trying to turn frustration into humor.

Dad's toolbox was a mess. He had every single box wrench except the one we needed. He thought that might have been the one he lost in the field. Whatever the case, I left him there, thumbing through the metal. I was deter-mined to get that tractor taken apart so we would be ready to put the new part in upon Mom's return. I stepped into the truck and headed to Glen Cooper's.

Glen lived four miles away, at the end of the road. He was always a savior in times like this. I found him in his shop, full of old engines that he spent his spare time rebuilding. Once he'd built an entire car from random old parts. He called it the Cooper. I poked my head in the door. "Glen?" I called out in my sweetest voice.

He looked up from his work and stared at me through his big square glasses. It had been a while since he'd come by to poke around my house site. Glen lived about as far out as you could get and was well known for shooting at trespassers on the gravel road beyond his gate. That is, if his dogs didn't flatten their tires when they stopped briefly to consider the

"No Trespassing" sign. I was always a little scared of him. But he cracked down on the cheap cowboys in black Bailey hats who pilfered hay from our barn in the winter, and we appreciated that.

"Charlene said you needed a tool," he said without any particular kindness.

I had called ahead to warn him I was coming and had talked to his wife on the phone. "Sure do," I said as I headed in. "A ⁹⁄₁₆" box wrench with a cheater."

He walked over to his toolbox—not your average toolbox, which is a bundle of bullshit and invariably will not contain what you need. This box was so tall I could have walked right into it if all the drawers were taken out. Each drawer had a label: *Wrenches, Screwdrivers, Clamps, Sockets, Pliers, Vice Grips*, etc. And inside, the tools were perfectly organized by size, from pieces smaller than my pinkie to others bigger than my arm.

"Yeah, I've got a few of those." He fingered through the ⁹⁄₁₆" box-wrench pile and handed me one that was imprinted with the words *Made in China*. "You can have this one. How much cheater do you need?"

"About a foot."

"I can make it longer. If you're gonna cheat, you want as much leverage as you can get."

I considered it, but knew I only had room for a short one. "No, a short one will do this time."

We walked out to his pipe pile, where every size, shape, length, and metal lay in ordered rows. When I say walk, I mean he walked and I ran. He pushed off the outside of his heels and seemed propelled by his forward lean. He grabbed

131

what I needed and blew back to his shop. He set it in a device that I did not recognize at first, but it ripped through the pipe in an instant. Sparks flew. I hid behind the door. He slipped the wrench in, turned around, and held it out to me.

Without a smile, he said, "You keep that, ya hear."

"Thanks, Glen," I said to his back, as he returned to his workbench. Trotting out to my truck, I felt so thankful. The support felt familiar, something I'd never felt anywhere else in the world. Between the wretched weather and the travails of my building project, I had the ticket to knowing my neighbors, mostly because I lacked ego completely and was willing to ask for help.

When I got home, Dad was sanding the breast of one of the massive wooden women in his shop. He set the tool down, peeled off his goggles, and unplugged his ears. "Did you get the wrench?"

"Sure did," I said with a little attitude, quite pleased with myself.

"I've always been too scared to go down there to Glen's place," he said as we walked toward the tractor, which was parked in the driveway just beyond Dad's shop.

We pushed back into the side of the tractor together with the new tool. "I know. You always made me scared to go down there, too. But he's nice. He just gave me the part," I said.

"Gave it to you?!" Dad whipped around to look at me, nearly whacking his head. "You mean he doesn't want it back?"

"Nope, he had about a dozen of them and couldn't believe we didn't even have one," I laughed, thinking about Dad's toolbox.

"Oh great, now he's going to think I'm even more inept than he already did. That man is a real farmer. He's the kinda guy that loves this shit," Dad said with a laugh and a crooked face, because, Lord knows, he sure didn't love this shit. We were still crammed in the side of the tractor, trying out our new tool.

I wanted to tell him, "You're missing out, Dad, on *this* place and its people," but I refrained. "He sure does. I really like that about him," I said instead.

It was becoming clear to me that I couldn't learn everything about this place from my Dad. I would need people like Glen and Travis to teach me about farming and mechanics, weather and tools. What I didn't know yet was that only my father could teach me how to survive the desert for a lifetime. Not by his successes, but by his failures.

THE THIN BLUE LINE

D espite the hurry the day before, we had to wait several days because the tractor part had to be ordered. In the meantime, Mom schooled me in log building. She told me about an uncle who lived in a log cabin in the San Rafael Valley in Colorado. In the summer the cabin was ideal, cool and comfortable, but the first snows of November blew in like white dust. The gaps between the logs were not obvious when you looked, but the air blowing through could put out a match. The snow sifted in like sugar and piled up on his floor.

The physical act of putting logs together isn't hard. There are two main activities: scribing and notching (essentially measuring and cutting), and like any sort of construction, there are bad measurements and bad cuts. Such mistakes are not only immensely frustrating, but result in snow blowing into the house.

Scribing is not an ideal activity for cold weather. The basic act of scribing is to clutch a small instrument and hold perfectly still while your boots freeze to the ground. The scribe is a delicate aluminum tool that looks a lot like a protractor. There are two levels to monitor its position—side to side and up and down. The bottom arm of the V is metal and comes to a sharp point that is dragged along the bottom log. The top of the scribe is an ink pencil, which marks the log to be cut. The scribe translates a mirror image of the bottom log onto the belly of the log above it. The bottom of every log is then excavated with a chain saw, or notched, until the logs fit together perfectly. Ultimately the disparity between a warm house and a cold house is directly related to the thin blue line of ink, its accurate placement and then precision in removing material exactly to the line.

After days spent with the tractor torn apart, Dad and I got it put back together and gassed it up. The day was cold and light, not freezing or bright. The ground was soft and moist under our feet, not sloppy. Just another winter day. We're standing back from the fumes, Dad in his insulated overalls and wool hat that I knitted him, his flat-bottomed boots and Von Zipper sunglasses that I had given him years ago. And, of course, his crucifix, hanging on a long chain around his neck, was sneaking out from under his neck gator.

"Now, Seer, you gotta check all the bolts that hold your rig together. I had a tire come right off the other day," he said, kicking the tire.

"I know. The tie rod on my truck that holds the front end together came apart, and my tires were turned in opposite directions. Thank God it happened in a parking lot and not at eighty miles an hour."

"Jesus! Sar. Did you go to the altar and give a donation immediately?"

"What? We've never gone to church except for holidays. I've never given a donation, and I've never seen you give one either. You're not even religious."

He interrupted me. "Hell yes, I'm religious. What do you think I've got this thing around my neck for?" He squinched his face. "I may not go to church, but I'm a true Christian. I just spend my whole life repaying the grace I receive. But sometimes you gotta do something big when you've been spared. I'd be broke if I paid every time I was spared." He shook his head wildly with a squeak and tried to get back on track. "In any case, not to make too fine a point, I am completely in touch with my own failures and those of society, and every other damn thing for that matter. And I'm just living to make up for it all. It's as clear as this diesel dripping down the side of this here tractor." He climbed up to peer down into the hole and top it off. "That'll do," he said.

I closed the valve on the tank and took the nozzle from him so he could climb down. He blew my mind sometimes with those little diatribes that came out of the blue. It left me wondering what to make of him, and I had to start over in my efforts to understand him.

He climbed up the back of the tractor and plopped down in the seat. To my relief, the tractor fired up without too much time on the glow plug. He drove up from the heart of the ranch, where equipment is parked near the gas tanks and tools, to the log decks where I had chosen four logs for the day. One by one, with Dad on the tractor, we guided them up from the decks to the house. The house was feeling a little like a pyramid, one massive block being moved at a time. Dad lined up with the wall receiving the log, then waited while I gathered my blocks and poles. Each log had to be perched on square blocks so that it sat level over the log beneath it. So if each log has a fat end and a skinny end, then the skinny end needed a large block under it and the fat end needed a little block. And the final placement needed to be secured with cross boards to keep the log from falling.

Dad shifted in his little metal seat and pulled his hat low. He looked agitated, maybe by the gray cold, or by the building, or by the fact that he was even at the ranch. With his hunched, don't-ask-too-much-of-me posture, he looked like he was reaching a breaking point. I felt horribly selfish, but I just jumped back down to the end of the log and put my hands on it as he lifted it off the ground with the tractor. Then we worked together to guide the log into position on its blocks.

Dad eased the log off the ground while I held it steady. He inched the tractor forward, careful not to pop the clutch and jerk things. We set the log down tentatively with Dad hovering on the hydraulics so the tongs wouldn't lose tension and let the log roll off its blocks. This moment was stressful every time, with the log in such a delicate balance, especially since I'd had a couple of logs fall on me and the higher they got, the more nerve-wracking it became. I hurried around, checking the log's aspect and making sure it was perfectly in line with the rest of the wall. It would be easy to mess up and set each log a little farther to the outside until the wall had a serious lean. But the whole process was just eyeballed, nothing precise about it. Just my style. After many slight adjustments, I jumped down and grabbed my long pole. I nailed one end into the log and the other into the floor of the house to stabilize the log. At that point Dad lowered the tongs so I could free them from the log, and he headed back to the decks to line up with the next log.

We set several logs with the tractor, then blocked and tacked them into position so that I could scribe them. Then we took down the logs I had already scribed for Dad to notch while I scribed the newly set logs. The goal was to get us both in a position to work for a few hours without having to fire up the tractor to shift logs, a constant shuffle that went on for five straight months.

After the log shuffling, Dad and I worked together on a short bit of log that we could move without the tractor, but that we were having trouble fitting. Together we could tip the log up to cut little pieces off the notch, which were keeping the log from sitting down snug. Dad's idling chain saw sent a sharp vibration into my floor, which reverberated up through my boots and out into my fingers; it shook my frozen digits in a way that made me sure they were still there. We had just tipped up that little four-foot log for the sixty-third time. I was counting. I stood and wondered at what point we should just give up and get another log.

"A little more here, and that'll be it."

I am sure that Dad said just a little more would do it, oh, maybe, forty-some times. I probably scribed it poorly, and then Dad didn't take enough out of the notch for the log to fall down snug. We worked on that log for the better part of three hours. I stood there listening to the drone of the saw through my earplugs. For the first half of the process we were both looking, wiggling, feeling, sure of what needed to be shaved back to fix the problem. At some point I pulled my hat down lower and my neck gator up so that they nearly met over my safety goggles. Only a sliver of clear plastic at my eyes was exposed. I committed myself to the long haul toward perfection.

Dad was certainly engaged in the fine-tuning of this log. Usually he deferred to me. Not that he liked to be ordered around, but he would generally rather be told what to do than be the lead man. It was during rare times like this that I saw my father's capacity for doing a job absolutely and correctly. He is the example I follow when I muster the energy to do a job right no matter what it takes.

Dad turned off his chain saw. "There."

Snow rolled across the floor like tiny marbles, and my oiled canvas pants cracked as I bent over to look at the log. "Looks great," I said through my neck gator.

"Lunch?"

"Yep." Every utterance took effort, so we kept them short.

Chyulu crawled out of the pile of tarp he had buried himself in, and we walked stiffly back to the house. We didn't need to take off our boots once we got there. The ground was too hard to pick up any dirt. We moved straight to the woodstove, stoked it, and stood six inches from it for a good ten minutes before either of us could say anything.

"I think the log moved a little when I was scribing." I looked at my feet to see if they were still there. My boots had taken to insulating the cold.

"Yeah, that notch was too shallow." He paused to stroke Chyulu's head, who leaned closer, soaking up the touch. "It's good not to waste any log."

"Four feet. Eight dollars. I don't know, I think we could have afforded to just start over."

There wasn't anything else to say about that little log. Dad turned to face the stove and said, "This weather makes me think about Mexico. I bet the blue board would want to catch some waves."

I'd been hearing this a lot. "Yeah, I bet," I offered. I didn't want to tell him I felt the same way.

"I'm not going to stay here another winter," he said and pushed his hands into his pockets. His brow furrowed like he'd made up his mind and things were going to change.

This conviction was new for my father. He had spent his entire adult life vacillating. He would adamantly lobby for gear he needed in order to get away to the beach. He needed a camper so he could stay cheaply on the Oregon coast, waiting for surf. He needed a different wetsuit or surf setup. He would stand on one side of the argument and then the other, arguing at the same time for and against himself. In his loaded mind he suddenly didn't need the camper at all, or he didn't want to go without my mother. He wore us out, wanting Mom and I to give credence to his ideas, but it was always just a cycle of the rising and dashing of hopes. Nothing ever materialized. But Mexico seemed different, with that blue board navigating to the other side of his stoned detachment from reality.

Turning to him, I said, "Thanks for not leaving me this winter."

"Yeah, this is the last time you're going to get this kind of work out of me, this time of year." Standing there in front of the woodstove in his coveralls and jacket and heavy boots and leather gloves, covered in shavings and grease and dirt and snow like he'd materialized right out of the ground, I couldn't imagine this place or this stove without him.

Looking at him for a long time, I tried to erase him from his shop and his truck and his field and his dogs, and I couldn't. He lived here, like no one lives anywhere else. His mind and his little body contained a living history of this particular spot on the planet. A billion treadless boot prints. A million puffs of blue smoke. Suddenly Mexico, for months of the year?

"This place won't be the same without you," I said finally.

"I've been building your kingdom for a lifetime, Sarah, and this place will have you. I need the sea."

I didn't say anything else. I just received the news and leaned against my parent's log wall, looking out at the snow hitting the window.

After lunch I put on a couple of extra layers, which filled out the space between my body and my outer canvas layer and felt like a full body cast. Dad and I reluctantly stepped out the back door.

"I was wondering if maybe you would rather read by the fire for the afternoon and I could work on my art," Dad said while we stood on the little back step together, the door closed behind us, neither of us stepping off. He was testing me.

"No," I said. "I want to work on that house."

I was proving, to him and myself, that I could work the ranch no matter the task or the weather. That I could keep moving despite the cold, like he had for the better part of thirty years. That I could trudge through the slowest winter hours and earn my dinner. What I wondered to myself was whether I could work the ranch alone, without my dad, and if that was the best way to live out my days. I didn't have an answer. My house was just a short stack of logs, but a warm, quiet shelter floated in my head, and that image kept me going.

We made the trek back to the house site and before long I could hear Dad's saw ring into a log around the south side of the house, still in disbelief that we were back on the job after our morning's efforts. It had been cold for days and didn't look like it was going to ease off. You could call it "frigid" or "freezing" or "chilly" or "frosty" or "bitter," but really it was just flat-out cold. I had a contractor friend who wouldn't build when it dropped below -10 degrees. Just wouldn't. He said the machines couldn't deal with it. It wasn't below -10 degrees, so Dad and I just lumbered through the days, mind over matter. He had spent his entire adult life on the ranch, 365 days a year. He didn't talk about it. He didn't tell stories about the cold or how tough he was. He didn't tell me I hadn't even seen cold yet, like most men I knew. He just walked out the door every morning and stayed out there all day long. He was well into another tank of gas while I slouched on the tailgate of the truck taking short, infrequent breaths and thinking. Dad hadn't stalled when he walked over to his saw. He pulled his goggles down, choked it, and pulled the cord. I finally picked up my scribe and walked to my log.

Cold seeped through my clothes and skin, into my bones. It locked my hands onto the legs of the scribe and I inched along, my eyes fixed in front of me. The tension in my eyes, neck, and jaw seemed to hold the levels as I moved slowly down the log. Periodically I threw my head back and shrugged off the tension that made my neck ache, peeled my feet off the frozen ground and set them back down. My mind stepped out of the back of my head and I wondered if Dad's mind had wandered off to the sea, beyond the bitter day and the drone of the saw, his blue board tucked under his arm. My mind rambled through its own stories of water, jumping from continent to continent.

As the flat gray sky slowly eased toward darkness, Dad and I came to a stopping point—my log scribed, his log notched. We loaded our tools and piled into the truck, the broken doors rattling down the gravel road since they hadn't fully shut since the '80s.

"Why haven't you been running, Sarah?" Dad asked.

"No time, I guess. Too tired. Too dark," I responded. I had always liked to run. Not fast or competitively, but just down the dirt road to loosen up enough to stretch. I had been thinking about starting up again, since the construction felt so hard on my body; something about anaerobic, heavy-lifting work, in heavy canvas clothes, was hard on a girl.

"Well, it will be dark again by the time we're done feeding, but I'd ride my bike along if you wanted to run. Keep you company, and maybe safe from the cougars," Dad offered with a laugh.

I thought for a minute. This was a rare offer from my dad. "Yeah, I'd like that," I said finally and turned to him with a smile.

We split up the feeding, and then I changed into my running clothes. Dad was waiting on his bike when I ran out the back door. He was still fully clad. He took a hit and we rolled down the driveway to the road. I called for Chyulu and extended my stride. It felt so good to be free of my layers and tools and heavy boots.

"Yeehaa!" Dad yelled as he came whizzing past. "Faster, Seer," he squealed. "Can you hear it?"

"No! What?"

"It's a dragon on the wing! Fire blasting out its nose. Swoosh . . . Watch the tail!" He hooted as he got his little legs whipping his bike pedals around.

I laughed and ran harder.

"That's it, Sar, let 'er rip."

Dad had read *The Lord of the Rings* aloud to me when I was a child, and he would create new scenes and characters as I ran—long, detailed scenes with fantastic motivation and unbearable suspense. Into the story he would drop little gems of wisdom, such as "Time and tides wait for no one." Sometimes his aphorisms would require a bit more deciphering: "Don't get hung up on the criticality of your fiascos." "You have to excavate your faith like dinosaur bones." "I kept you alive, and now you are tough as nails. There are no limits to what you are capable of." And that's why I was there, because I thought he might have the key to life's mysteries, somewhere in his foggy, stoned mind. I had spent my whole life growing weary of the stoned antics, eventually tuning him out. But now I was listening. Recording the gems. Thinking on his quips for days.

We ran a couple of miles out on the dirt road by moonlight, ducking and racing monsters of all sorts—his dynamic little voice carrying into the night, chirps and squeaks and giggles and dramatic inflection. I loved him most when he felt playful—lighthearted and hilarious.

After we turned around, we raced on the home stretch to the driveway.

"Pour it on, Seer! Dig it deep for the home stretch!" he yelled, pedaling as hard as he could.

I came to a winded stop at the end of the driveway, and he circled back to me.

"Right on, Sar. That's the kinda shit you need to shed this hard, heavy work." He reached out and slapped me on the back.

He was right. And after that, he biked along most nights while I ran. We could kick off the challenge of construction and enter a world of make-believe to finish our day.

HOW TO SURVIVE

One February evening, after a long day flailing away at the house, I drove into town to check my e-mail at the library. We didn't have Internet service at the ranch, and I loved that. I loved that I could disappear there. Even my cell phone barely got service. While I was online, I checked the surf forecast for the Oregon coast. A nice clean swell was predicted to roll in. I sat back in that big cushy chair and thought for a second. My hands in my lap looked dry and cracked. I was stiff in all my clothes and overheating a bit. I peeled my wool hat and scarf off and tried to smooth my hair. I wasn't used to being like this. I had been wearing bikinis and sun hats, shorts and T-shirts, and I was always clean from the river. Now, every line in my hands was full of dirt and oil. It was time for a break.

I drove home slowly, like I always did, just taking time to look around, to see what my neighbors were up to. My life had gotten so buried on the ranch, I barely raised my head to breathe. When I rolled into the driveway, I was surprised not to see my dad in his shop. He had gone to town for his annual haircut, and to make a trip to the gas station, since the farm truck was almost empty and we saved the fuel at the ranch for tractors. But he had left ages ago. He should have been back and the horses fed, but they just nickered over the fence. I grew worried.

Unlike almost everyone else in the world, he didn't have a cell phone, so I called the lady that cut his hair. He'd missed his appointment. I jumped into my truck and headed to town. We lived exactly ten miles from the town of Terrebonne, at the end of the narrow, windy Lower Bridge Road. I looked down into the Deschutes River canyon, wondering if he'd gotten so frustrated that he'd run himself off the road. But he'd made it past the ravine. Instead, I found him at a bend in the road, the old red Chevy Cheyenne pulled onto the shoulder with its hood up. Dad was just beyond the truck, toiling over a long pile of basalt rocks. He was in the process of lashing two sticks together with some sage bark. They formed a cross. As I approached, he wedged the cross at the head of the pile of rocks. I stopped and waited while he looked down at the little grave where he'd buried himself, there on the side of Lower Bridge Road. It was a low point.

"How are you?" I asked.

"I don't like that question, Sar." He shook his head. "It's a modern question for modern people, and I'm living in the past. 'How are you doing?' is some bullshit question from Nancy Reagan. Everyone asks it, and they don't want to hear the real answer. So spare me."

I didn't say anything in return. It wasn't the time for a quick answer. I just made a mental note to myself: don't ask how he is doing.

Eventually he turned to me, "Thanks for coming," he said.

"Yeah. No problem. I was worried when you weren't home."

He dragged his feet as he walked toward me and the truck. "I guess I'll have to go to town another time. Did you bring a tow chain?"

"Of course," I said and grabbed it out of the back of the truck. I didn't even ask what the problem was. I just pulled in front of the old Chevy and hooked it up. Before we loaded up for the slow pull home, I said, "I was looking at the surf report, and it's supposed to be good later this week. I really think we should take a break and go."

"Yes. Please take me to the beach, Sar. I don't even care anymore if your mother can go. That blue board and me really need some time together."

I smiled and stepped in the truck, turning the key. I wanted to see if a couple of days with the sea could help him to be happier at the ranch. I too was frustrated with my project, and the cold, and was searching for the key to balance.

We pulled up the drive and dropped the Chevy off at the shop. After feeding the animals, we lifted the hood to see what the problem was. Always check the battery connection first. A poor connection is the number one reason a vehicle won't start. As I twisted the positive cable to see if it was tight, it just snapped off. The whole copper cable was green with corrosion. Luckily, we always had a spare.

I put my safety glasses on and scooted under the truck while Dad fetched the cable. The gravel broke loose from the frozen ground under my canvas back. I had to unbolt the cable from the starter, and after taking a look, I discovered I needed a ⅝" socket to get it off.

Dad was peering down through the engine at me. "What do you need?"

"A ⅝" socket, please."

He fetched it from the toolbox and was back looking at me through the engine. "One time my Dad asked me for a wrench when he was under a truck, just like you are now. And without thinking, I just dropped the tool to him."

I scrunched my face, wondering what was about to happen to me.

"Well, you can imagine what happened from the vantage point you have now. The wrench hit him square in the nose, and he couldn't move to miss it." He laughed at himself. "I am such an idiot."

"Maybe you could hand it to me down here on the ground," I said.

"Of course," he said. "But it's times like these that you get to ask yourself: Who is your dad? Who was his dad? And who are you?"

He handed me the wrench and I took my gloves off for dexterity. The cold steel burned my fingers.

"We've got thirty battery poles around here, and I just can't keep track of them all. Just have to fix them when they fail," he said, explaining himself from up top.

"It's true," I said as I fumbled along.

"In Mexico people ask, 'Que onda?' What do you own?" he said, as he did some push-ups off the front of the truck. "They are seeking an emotion. What guilt do you own? You own your state of being in a bigger dimension. 'How' is so specific to ourselves, it's ridiculous."

I was just lying under the truck at that point, listening.

"The earth is our trial period, Sarah. And brief it is, the time we have to experience the flesh. This is the place where spirits interact. Here, we contact each other and fix our trucks and shit."

I laughed a little at that. The sky beyond his little brown face and wild white eyebrows was a darker gray. The limbs of the apple tree were shifting just above him. The cold seeped into my back.

"The flight of the soul can never ever be expunged. This is the hammer zone of eternity. It knocks us about the head and ears until we can interact with God. We're being cleaned and scrubbed. Some people go early. God will rip a five-year-old right off this earth, because mercy is an incredible force and death its best vehicle. The corpse is just a vessel, Sar. We're living on a tilt, cognizant about the woes of the world. It's better to die for something than to live for nothing." He pulled out his pipe and took a hit, then said, "Let us stand in the way of our own filth and addictions. Our Latin neighbors are waiting for some sign of comprehension of our mortality."

I waited for a few minutes, looking up at him through that greasy engine. He looked into the distance. Finally, I felt like it was safe to come out. That he had said his piece.

At the end of the week, I hid from the wind behind a piece of driftwood and watched Dad get tubed inside a cold northern Pacific wave. The saltwater was crusty in my eyebrows and lashes after I got schooled in the surf for a couple of hours and gave up. The heat of the day dwindled around two o'clock, the sun and the wind canceling each other out. Yakina Point jutted off the central Oregon coast and caught a sweet little northwest swell that peeled right before it closed out way down the beach. My parents and I had come to this beach since I was a small child. I can still see myself running naked through the water in a little green knit hat, losing my sense of balance when the water rushed around my feet.

I motivated myself for another round of surf and paddled out beyond the breakers to where Dad sat. The Oregon coast in February is brutally cold, but the surf is good. My wet-suit kept my body warm, but the saltwater on my face was as cold as liquid can be without freezing. As I approached, Dad smiled and said, "Saltwater is the closest thing to human blood." His face had eased into a serenity that I hadn't seen in years. Dad was in the midst of such clear revitalization. I wondered if this act of stealing away from the desert was the answer to how to survive there. Would it be enough, a few days here and there? Dad spun and paddled hard for a wave, gracefully standing, and left me there atop his old Dusty Rhodes surfboard that he got in high school. I looked out at the sea, waiting for another mound of water to build into a wave, and thought about how learning to ride on the backs of rivers seemed like a fluid progression from riding on the backs of horses and ocean waves. Could I go back to just horses and the sea, sprinkled between long days at the ranch? I loved the way the sea made me feel so small. I loved the way the water went out of the sand under my feet. I loved the way a wave combed through black rocks polished round and pulled them toward the sea. I loved the birds that spilled around me like water spills around a rock in the river.

The ocean was the first place I was humbled. As a child, I learned to go limp instead of resisting the sea.

Horses were the other force that guided me in this world. I didn't grow up with other kids; I grew up with horses. My first was Roany the Pony, then Charlie the Rocket Ship. When I was five, my mom gave me a big black gelding that was born at the ranch. I named him Smoke Rose, until we recognized his oral fixation and called him Nipper. I broke ponies for a neighbor in batches of three, and as payment he would give me one to sell. It was a good deal, and a lot of work, but even as a ten-year-old I always had money. I saved several thousand dollars to buy an elephant until my mom finally broke the news to me that no matter how much money I saved, we would not be buying an elephant. So I used the money for college. But there were more special horses.

One day when I was fourteen, I was poking through the sagebrush and juniper trees, lying on my tummy for a close look at the tiny yellow flowers that blanket the wet, sandy earth that time of year. I noticed a filly's muzzle amid the yellow blanket flung before me. She looked intently at my gingerbread body clad in canvas, and then her wide eyes caught my own. Her left eye was striking—half brown and half blue like the globe. A forest billowed from the center. She was a sorrel paint, her coloring like white lace draped over red earth.

I bought that wild filly from my neighbor and named her Meridian. The first time I sat down carefully into the saddle, I felt slung up by the tension of an inexperienced back, but we moved out lightly across the ground and she carried me willingly. Throughout my high school years we explored from our home in the Lower Bridge Valley. We knew every sandy draw, rocky hillside, open field, white dune, and narrow creek within a day's ride. We covered ground in the early mornings and late afternoons at wild speeds, weaving through brush and rocks.

After high school I left for college, and Meridian stayed home. It didn't take long for me to miss her, so I fetched her over a school holiday. I found a place to board her close to school and close to some wheat fields where we could ride. When the sun hovered over the horizon like it does in late spring, Meridian ate her grain and pushed the metal bowl around on the ground. She stood still while I brushed the dirt off her and picked her feet. I swung my saddle onto her back and cinched up. Climbing on, we headed west, and I thought about my mother, who was always with me when I eased into a saddle, the same way my father was with me whenever I was on the water. Mom had a way of communicating with horses so gently and clearly that they always did what they were asked. I didn't ask much, and in a way, I got similar results.

I let Meridian lead, and we danced as seasoned partners would. She trotted to the corner and took a hard right into the fields. She slowed for the descent into the first trough of land. I responded by leaning back to counter gravity until we started up the other side. She ran and I stood in my stirrups, poised over her back so that she could reach under herself and move easily. We were headed to where the only two fences meet and there is a hole, which is the access to the distance. From there we loped for miles along combine tracks, always toward the setting sun. I loved that the sky was half of our world.

We rode fast out through the field until Meridian stopped at the highest point around. She stood still, facing the horizon. She did not eat. A huge flock of blackbirds bounced in the wheat stubble in the distance. A low haze glowed orange and took the texture out of the land that reached before us. The eye of the sun finally blinked, and at that moment Meridian turned toward home and took off at a run. Cold air hovered in the low spots between harmonic, rolling hills. We got lost in the earth's creases, the sky turning slowly from east to west. The crystal blue of night swallowed the creamy blue of day. Meridian was an adventure. She knew the way to wonder and mystery. I followed by opening myself to what she had to teach me: the lesson was simply one of presence.

What I found in rivers lay somewhere between this presence I discovered with Meridian and the humbling nature of the sea. I had had little experience with rivers as a child. I did not grow up on a river. There was only an irrigation ditch that my dad and I paddled our surfboards up in the summer to stay in shape for the big winter swells at the beach. My parents took me on a rafting trip for my twelfth birthday and our guide's name was Elvis. But that day, when I traveled a river as if it were a carnival ride, was not the reason I became a river guide. The shift from saltwater to freshwater and from horses to rivers was driven by my subconscious obsession with vulnerability, something that became clear on the Colorado River at Lava Falls.

A river flows along the path of least resistance. Not me. I had to learn a new path, or meet the river's power head on. When the current took me in its constant flow, I learned by feeling. Downstream, its body curved and swung around great bends and over massive rocks. By paying attention and committing its every move to memory, the water became predictable. Through miles and miles of canyons, the river let me learn to read it. Finally, I simply responded to it, moving more of the time with the water pulling downstream than against it. The river took over and brought me along on the journey it dictated, unfolding before me into new configurations and hydraulics, and I followed with greater and greater ease.

There was no place I felt more alive than in the presence of a free-flowing river. Just the movement of the stream running through my college campus captured me. Sitting on the bank or driving by at eighty miles per hour, I scouted my line. When I saw a river, I felt it. It pulled my eyes to where it wanted to run—I could feel it in my body. Rivers marked my path and gave me coordinates on the planet; each place was distinguished by its nearest flowing water. Idaho was the soft green of the Lochsa and its sweet smell of high mountain water. Arizona was the light blue of the Little Colorado, like a frozen glacial cave in early morning light, mixing with deep emerald green at its confluence with the great Colorado River. It was knowing, even in the dark, that there had been rain upstream by the pungent smell of fresh soil in the water.

Looking out at the sea on that cold winter day, as my dad headed out for another ride, I remembered how I glowed in the shadow of something as great as the sea or a horse or a river. Moving with an animal at a run, bareback with my arms flung to the wind, hair loose and whipping, is how I would describe my childhood. Twelve-hundred-pound animals pulling across the ground at a dead run dictated my life for twenty-one years. And then, following that, thousands of cubic feet of water ripping through canyons had taken hold. I thrived when I was out of control. I was afraid, and the challenge was to let go. The crux of my obsession was at the moment when I couldn't go back, when I had hopped onto something that I could not stop.

As a wave formed, I turned and paddled to catch it, cold water slipping between my skin and the rubber of my wetsuit. Reaching for my first strokes, I thought about finding this kind of energy at the ranch, something to hold me over between river trips. Something that could keep me fulfilled. It had been a long time since my last ride, but I decided to look to my horse like a desert wave or a river moving across dry ground. As the wave lifted beneath me, I jumped to my feet and cruised all the way to shore. Standing on the edge of the place where the earth meets the sea, I watched my dad sail in on another long ride.

CONDUIT

Hundreds of creatures make their homes on the ranch, from eagles in their nests to black widow spiders in their holes. Starlings live in the ancient lightning-struck juniper to the west of my house. In the early summer, a chorus of hungry voices comes from the hollow center of the tree. The hay field is open to deer, elk, coyotes, hawks, falcons, eagles, owls, ants, gophers, spiders, butterflies, ladybugs, snakes, mice, grasshoppers, and worms. At different times I've seen them all as I lap the twenty-five acres on the old red Farmall tractor during farming season. When my headlights catch dust in the air, I know the horses are running.

There is a distinct order to the land between the sagebrush and juniper—animal trails wind along like the worn paths on the carpet in our house. I know the mule deer will cross the road at the Long Hollow irrigation pond in the evening. I always slow when I round the bend on my way home, because I know the deer will need water after a day on the rim above the ranch. After they drink, they head back to the orchard grass field, passing my south window on the way. Dad will take one in the fall and the mountain lions will take a few more.

The mountain lions on our side of the river live in the basalt cliffs that brace the Deschutes River. They don't give us any trouble, but the lions across the river on the Warm Springs Reservation kill several calves and colts every year. The ravens do their share, too, descending upon newborns, pecking them to death. They work together like a pack of dogs to distract the cow and attack the calf. But it's the cats people worry about. Hunting parties claim they saw a dozen cougars in broad daylight on the open reservation. I had ridden almost every day for twenty years, but I'd never seen a lion. Every time I rode my horse off the place, I went with hopes of seeing a big cat, despite Dad telling me, "She'll eat your dog."

At the end of February, the snows flew again and the temperature dropped below zero, which the wind whipped down to a bitter forty below. Dad and I stepped into our gear and got out to the forty horses early in the morning. We found them on the leeward sides of the thickest juniper trees. They faced south. Dad sat behind the steering wheel of the old red truck, with the window cracked so he could hear me as I fed hay out the back. Chyulu held his place on the top of the hay pile while I threw every flake of hay under the trees for protection. Chaotic wind currents slung dry grass into my eyes. The horses ran across the dry-ground flats as if blown by the wind. It caught their manes and tails when they ran perpendicular to the gusts and billowed their bodies like sails as they tried to maintain their course.

After I'd fed the horses and broken the ice in the water troughs, Dad stepped out of the truck and lumbered to the mudroom. Chyulu bounced off the haystack and followed him while I gathered loose strings in a gunnysack. Chyulu rushed to his water bowl, nosed it, then looked up at Dad, who had paused to watch him from the step. Dad had set out hot water for Chyulu before we left to feed the horses. It was now frozen. He bent down slowly, picked up the dish, and walked inside. I moseyed to the woodpile to split kindling. From there, I watched Dad set fresh water out with some food. Then he strode to his shop. We usually planned what we'd do on the house after feeding was done, but when Dad intentionally walked past me, he was making it clear that he was unwilling to entertain the idea of another day of cold work in a bitter wind. I didn't blame him, and I didn't follow him to his shop to pester him about it. I finished the kindling and wandered out to the geldings' pasture.

Trucks, saws, and tractors won't run when it's that cold, but a horse will. Meridian was laid up with a hurt leg, so I turned to my favorite old gelding. Nipper had finished his breakfast and was drinking from his trough before it froze again. I grabbed his bridle off the dead juniper branch; then I opened the gate and he stepped out. He lifted his muzzle to my face, the alfalfa sweet on his breath. He stood still while I put his bridle on, knocked the dirt off his back with my gloved hand, and threw my right leg over. I didn't need a saddle since his thick winter coat held me tight to his back. I settled in and gave him a nudge with my calves.

Just across the road from the ranch is where my backyard extends onto public land. The land tips east into the Deschutes

River drainage, starting with rivulets and washes, growing into dry draws and canyons; water falling on the desert over the ages and finding its way to the sea. On a dry winter day, the land held the ghost of water and Nipper and I followed its path past Meadowlark Mesa to the river. The Three Sisters brooding over my right shoulder looked as if they were made out of construction paper and pasted flat across the western horizon. Nipper usually swelled and burst down the trail like a black storm cloud, but today he slowed, bogged down in the deep snow. As we loped down the canyon, the juniper trees, having shed their film of dust in the fall rains, looked slightly more vibrant against the white backdrop. Red boulder faces, where the snow hadn't stuck, lined the canyon. We moved from memory, missing every rock and badger hole hidden in our path. Riding Nipper felt like riding a river. He moved like water. I thought for a moment that this massive animal could take the place, at least partially, of the river. He could keep me satiated in the desert.

We crossed four major deer trails and spooked a dozen jackrabbits, then blasted over the last rise to the river, stopping at the cliff edge. A couple hundred feet below, the water meandered, half frozen and slow, like black obsidian, unable to gather any color from the sky. Wine-colored dogwoods lined the banks. I thought about where the river could take me from that bend below us and wished for a second that it would carry me away. I was daydreaming about floating downstream when Nipper suddenly jumped and spun around. Like a conduit, his fear was electric, and I was firmly plugged in. A hundred yards downstream, a lion, low-slung and tawny, looked over its shoulder at the two of us as we fought over whether to stay or run. The cat lumbered casually with high steps through the snow, out to the head of land that built at the river bend. She wasn't in any hurry; her long fat tail barely cleared the snow. When she bent out of sight, we followed.

Nipper walked with short steps. His neck was stiff, and the tension in his back indicated I might be left in midair at any minute. The mountain lion disappeared into the rocks, and we continued, passing the point where we usually turned back, just before the ground gets too steep and ends abruptly in cliffs. I craned my head around to see where the cat had disappeared to, and then Nipper's feet slipped out from under him on the slick rock. His massive body pitched left onto my leg, and we started to slide. His barrel pinched me against the ground and dragged me across the rock and sagebrush. It felt like my leg was being pulled out of my hip. I grabbed his mane to stay with him and strained to see the edge of the cliff coming at us. A few feet from the edge, a ball of brush, snow, and mud stopped us. The instant we stopped, Nipper clambered to get up. I balled up under him to protect my head and legs, but he struck my lower left leg, and it felt like he was ripping my calf muscle off my bone. He spun around, and I grabbed for his reins, but he lunged up the hill and out of sight.

I felt around for blood under my insulated suit, but there was just blunt pain. I sat up and didn't have to lean forward at all to see straight down the cliff. Then the lion emerged from the rocks and my breath caught. She sat down on her haunches and looked at me. I looked for my horse. All the fears of the farmers and ranchers that I had scoffed at could be vindicated in this moment. Was she sizing me up? I was clad in oiled canvas, but it wouldn't have taken much to get at my warm flesh. She looked cold, the way she tucked her elbows in, and her fur was straight-out stiff. I was cold, too. My body was covered in snow. She was too far away for me to see the color of her eyes, but I'm sure she could see mine.

As dusk washed over us, I sat astonished at the length of the encounter. Without taking my eyes off hers, I realized we were of the same ground, giving to the same system. We crossed paths every day without me knowing it. We shared the bitter cold and the struggle for warmth and shelter. After days of freezing fog and hoarfrost, we would turn our faces to the same sun for another hot, dry summer, and shade would lie across our hides, giving us the same sense of relief.

Suddenly, the lion darted back into the rocks, and I turned to see my horse blasting hot air from his nostrils at the cliff corner. He looked like a dragon, the steam puffing out in columns. He was my first horse, and I was his only girl. He had taken me to an intersection and was responsible for retrieving me, despite his ornery, defiant nature. I crawled to him and struggled up onto his back and into the steam rising off him.

The moon rose as we headed home along the river. My leg ached against Nipper's side as I moved with his long strides. The rhythm and motion of the stride was reminiscent of the rock of a raft on a big river. I had imagined riding Nipper for many months and miles when I was on the Futaleufú River. Now here I was, and he felt so good despite the pain. I don't know what on earth had taken me so long to find him again. The house project had consumed me. I hadn't taken a break for five months, until Dad and I went to the beach. As we walked the canyon rim that night, I realized that by giving this horse a small piece of my day, he could carry me to the most terrifying and magical moments—just as terrifying and magical as any river.

FOREST HUSBANDS

S pring wore on and so did the house. I had started scribing faster than Dad could notch, which frustrated both of us. I wanted to learn to notch, but Dad didn't want to scribe while I ran the saw. He said it was too cold, which pissed me off. One night at the dinner table, Mom got fed up with our cheap shots, mostly about who was a bigger wuss about the cold.

"Shut *up*!" she yelled at us like we were a couple of kids, twenty-two and fifty going on fifteen. In a calm voice she said, "Maybe the notching process would speed up considerably if you were both working at it." We nodded and finished our meal in silence.

The next day, Mom found a used chain saw on Tradio, a swap-and-sell program that airs for an hour every morning on an AM station. I called the guy and he agreed to come out that evening after work. Dad and I finished the afternoon, him notching and me scribing. When the sun went down, we fed the horses and waited outside in the garage. Dad was playing his guitar in his cutoff wool gloves while I hit the punching bag when a truck pulled up.

A massive man, over six feet tall and maybe three hundred pounds, pulled the saw out of the back of his rig and stood in the red glow of his taillights. He drop-started the saw in one pull, its thirty-six-inch bar just off the ground. Dad and I stood there gaping at a safe distance. Any normal human being starts a saw on the ground, alternating the choke over the course of several pulls. This guy revved the engine, and the sparks bounced off the blade. He looked like he was straight out of *The Texas Chain Saw Massacre*. Dad and I looked on like children, elbowing each other in excitement.

When the man cut the engine, he handed the saw to me. The weight of it nearly pulled me to the ground, but I caught myself, pretending I could handle it, no problem. Dad ran into the house for the $200 the guy wanted for the saw. He'd bought it when he was logging full time a couple of years before for $1,200. He climbed back into his truck and left us giggling in the driveway. We walked into the mudroom and heaved the saw up onto the washing machine. The giant saw had a name engraved in the orange plastic over the motor. *Forest Husbands*.

The next morning, Dad waited on the other side of a log for my first plunge cut with the saw. The plunge cut initiates the notch. It's a hard cut because using the saw's tip can make it catch and kick the saw back into your leg or your head. Forest Husbands didn't have a kickback bar, which would normally cut the engine if the saw jumped, so Dad taught me how to mind the tip of my bar so I wouldn't lose control of the saw and cut my leg off. We decided that I could do the major excavations and full-length ripping with the big saw after I got ahead in the scribing; then Dad would carefully carve out to the blue line. He was an artist with his saw. Only he could be trusted to take the wood back to the blue line.

Unlike the guy in the taillights, I couldn't start the saw on my own, no matter how hard I yanked on the cord. Dad had to start it for me, but despite the blow to my self-esteem, I loved Forest Husbands. Dad thought the saw was crazy big, too big to use, so I strutted around pulling the trigger, saying, "Having trouble? Need me to cut that?" My scribing sped up considerably when I knew I'd be able to (a) run the saw when I finished, and (b) stay warm while doing it. The whole project really picked up speed, and I couldn't believe how fast we were setting logs. In some places, I couldn't even see over the walls anymore. Everything was going great until the temperature dropped again and we couldn't keep the ice out of the horse troughs.

Horses colic without water. Just a little dry hay can cause compaction if they cannot drink. The hay turns into a knot in their gut; they roll, twist their intestine, and die. We had six water troughs for forty horses that we boarded in the winter for a summer camp. Every morning after we fed them, before we could head to the house site for work, we broke ice. It was -4 degrees, and the rendering plant couldn't come until Monday. We had to put Salty down the night before, because she twisted her gut. She was tight under a tarp then, east of the house, her body poison to the dogs.

The house was circled by seven horse pastures, all with different collections of horses, mostly defined by dietary needs. The bulk of the herd lived to the west of the house, where I fed several bales off the back of the truck while Dad drove. When we finished, I jumped out with Chyulu and headed to the trough at the south end of the compound. Dad drove up to the house and started on the troughs behind the house. We moved counterclockwise and eventually got to the trough where the other had started.

I threw a stick for Chyulu, who ran gingerly across the frozen ground; then I kicked the metal rod that had frozen to the ground next to the heaping pile of ice chunks. Chyulu dropped his stick again at my feet and I picked it up as well as the rod, threw the stick, and stepped through the pole fence. The ice on the trough got a good three inches thick overnight, so I started around the edge, trying to break it free of the metal wall. As I moved around the metal tank, eight feet in diameter, my hands started to feel the burn of the icy steel rod despite my thick gloves. After I busted the ice at the edge, I broke the pieces in the middle until they were small enough to scoop out. If the ice wasn't scooped out, it would freeze again immediately.

I stepped to the pole fence, leaned the rod against it, threw Chyulu's stick, and grabbed the pitchfork. I shoveled ice chunks out in big sweeping motions toward a heaping pile that wouldn't melt until spring. The ice pieces clanked together, sometimes skittering out at Chyulu, who was waiting with his stick. I was careful to keep my pitchfork angled toward the ground so the icy water couldn't drip onto my hands or legs. Occasionally a large hunk fell back in the trough, splashing water in my face, which had a sobering effect every time and made me move slowly, balancing my ice.

As I circled around the ranch I came back around to the house, where Dad usually started his part of the ice-breaking. Sometimes he got sidetracked, so I checked the troughs and found them frozen. He had gone to put water in the troughs I had cleared. As I finished clearing the trough he should have cleared, he walked up to the fence and said, "Why didn't you clear down there?"

I whipped around. "Me? I broke my troughs. You're the one not doing your share."

"What?! I broke all my usual troughs and yours, too."

"Yeah?! So did I! You must not be scooping the ice out, then."

"I scoop every damn piece." He paused for a moment. "Well, did you break this trough here?" He pointed to the one right behind the house with a horse looking at it like it needed to be broken.

"Yes."

"Well, so did I. Broke it and cleared it."

We marched out, throwing the metal gate open and spooking the thirsty horse. Snow packed in his hooves, the horse teetered off like he was wearing high heels. We raced up and looked over the edge. The dang thing was frozen. Our gloved hands shot out at the same time to touch it, and we both hit solid ice. We looked at each other and hooted with laughter. But it didn't take long for the humor to subside. We ended up spending the entire day circling the place, breaking ice, so the horses wouldn't colic.

Mom talks about cold winters when she first came to central Oregon from the Willamette Valley nearly thirty years before. She had about three dozen horses in training and the standpipe faucets froze, the house froze, the barn froze. She had one standpipe buried in the ground where the water flowed. She carried water from that source in buckets to every horse. She carried it to the house, to the cows, to the dogs, all day long. Within ten minutes the bucket would be frozen too hard for a horse to break it with his muzzle. I imagine her wondering what the hell she'd left the Willamette Valley for, shaking her head with a five-gallon bucket in each hand.

A horse will not break ice with its hoof. They show absolutely no inclination to paw the inside of a trough, frozen or thawed, but Dad had seen cylinders through a foot of ice down to water where a horse had melted it with his breath. There is nothing better to do on a cold day than spin yarns about colder days. It's the only thing that made me feel less assaulted by the bitter cold that I sucked to my core with every breath.

Walking around the house, taking turns breaking and scooping, Dad told me stories about when we used to have the longhorns. They had been gone for several years now, after even my mother tired of cattle work. Dad had gone along with the cattle operation, but when they made even Mom short-tempered, the cattle had to go. She says it wasn't even the burden of her husband hating but tolerating the cattle just so she could live out her dream. No, it was the cattle—the way they busted fences and bawled and seemed wholly unmanageable. But for a long time, the herd drank out of the water left in the irrigation pond from summer.

"I had to cut the ice at the pond with the chain saw," he said, waiting for me to break some more ice. "Every day I cut farther into the pond, until I had a thirty-foot-long tunnel with five-foot ice walls. Only one cow could drink at a time. They would have to walk down the chute and then back out, because they couldn't turn around," he laughed.

I remember him coming home every day covered in the ice that the chain saw had blasted him with. Mom said he looked like the abominable snowman. We hadn't had sustained subzero temperatures and ice like that for years. It was like the winters when we could have skating parties; when Rufus, the old Saint Bernard, would pull me in the sled while my parents glided along.

The stories made me feel a little bit better, but generally I was mad at the cold for slowing me down. Everyone knows you can't change the weather, and it's not personal, but it felt personal. I cursed the degrees that had all gone south and the blowing snow as I peered out my window in the mornings. Maybe I should be doing something else with my dad, I thought—a surf trip, perhaps.

Winter just pushed me down, but when I walked out the door I shouldered into it. I felt like I'd earned those days when the sun came out just at the moment that my hands couldn't possibly hang on to the wild vibrations of the saw a moment longer and snot crystals blocked my nose. I would close my eyes and turn to the sun—the closest thing to grace. When Forest Husbands threw sawdust back at me and covered me like a snowman, I smiled and thought of Dad with the anxious herd of longhorns waiting behind him.

COLD AND SLOW

As the house-building project eased into March, the winter refused to back off. I felt like I had a week's worth of wood chips stuck in my eyeballs. A blustery wind seemed to blow from every direction, every day. The gusts made me clumsy. If there was a wood block to trip on, my feet would find it. I spilled bar oil all over my saw. I dropped my spray bottle repeatedly and had to climb down the ladder to fetch it. I fell off the ladder, which I stood higher on every day as each log was set. I set down the chisel and couldn't find it for the life of me. I forgot my safety glasses. I felt like a blundering idiot, and with my eyes full of grit I couldn't see a damn thing.

One morning, Dad and I met at the log decks for another big north-wall log. I dreaded those logs. They were the biggest in the deck, and something went wrong every time we tried to set them. I built up all the other walls in the house until I had to put another north log in. I couldn't see Dad, but I threw my thumb in the air so he could see it over the stinger. The log lifted slowly, and I tested the weight of the light end. I pulled it down easily and gave Dad a nod.

He set the tractor in second gear, let out the clutch, and eased forward. I cleared the log and swung the other end up and over the bitterbrush and started the swing to miss the house. I thought I could make it between the butt of the log and a tree, but when the tractor turned at the corner of the foundation, it pinched my body against the old juniper. I felt my rib cage roll with the flat end of the log, off bone and on to the soft part of my stomach, and then I felt my spine on the tree behind me. Dad was watching the other end of the log, and there was no air in me for a scream. As the tractor moved forward, the butt of the log pressed harder and then rolled off my body. I let go, and the log dropped to the ground.

Dad whipped around when he heard the log drop. "What happened?" he yelled.

I couldn't speak. I buckled over for a moment to catch my breath. I wasn't hurt. Just squeezed. I stood up and grabbed the end of the log, "Nothing. Just didn't judge the swing right."

Taking hold of the log, my hands felt like blocks, and I rubbed at the frozen snot in my nose. Dad was lifting the log while I stood inside the half-built house, my mind wandering around the room, marveling at our progress despite the weather. I felt like I was digging a well into my center, deeper and deeper, and the water was starting to pour in steadily. It was a well that I could draw upon for strength, patience, and perseverance. My thumb was absentmindedly in the air—where Dad could see it even though I couldn't see him—when I lost hold of the light end of the log. The heavy end fell, and the force against the log tongs forced them open. When the log hit the floor, the impact snapped through the plywood and jolted me as it came up through my feet. I stood stunned, my heart racing and my breath short, and looked over at Dad who had stood up on the tractor to see me. He shook his head but didn't say anything.

Now the log was on the inside of the house, six-foot walls all around it, and the stinger on the tractor couldn't reach in to pick the log back up. I stood there for a moment. The work was hard enough when we did it right. I let out a frustrated sigh through my teeth. Dad took a hit off his pipe. He didn't bother hiding it, and I didn't care. I heaved the log back under the tongs, then let out the chain that held the tongs so they could reach. When Dad lifted the stinger and the chain came tight, the balance wasn't right, but I manhandled the log up and over the wall and back out of the house to the ground where we could start over. I sat down on the log in a slump. Dad set the emergency brake on the tractor and stepped down. He stood in front of me, and I looked at the ground.

"Maybe we should take a break," he said.

"We don't have time. I have to go back to work on the river in a month." I could feel tears in my voice, so I stopped. I'd left the river because I knew I needed to build a home, but the reality was that I couldn't stay away forever, not yet, anyway. The river was where I made a living, and I still loved it. At any other time in my life I'd be looking forward to going, but this time I wasn't ready and felt terribly rushed. Dad and I had just started to find our groove. I was just young, trying to be everywhere at once, unable to commit fully to the ranch by saying no to all the other parts of my life.

Though I didn't want to leave, I did hate the logs over my head, and building the house had strung me out physically, emotionally, and mentally. I had urges to fling my saw to the ground when it wouldn't work, drop the grinder when I couldn't get the V-groove right, kick large blocks of wood that were in my way even though they were obviously going to wreck my foot, rev the engine on the truck when I killed it, and generally abuse things that caused me pain, even if it was self-inflicted. I had lost hold of the journey, and the destination was just making me rancorous. And honestly, that was part of my journey, what I felt like I had to get through before I could leave.

"The logs will be here when you get back," Dad said with a rare gentleness.

I knew they would. That's how everything worked at the ranch. If we didn't have time, we would just finish next season. Projects waited, and no one minded. But I couldn't imagine getting in a groove with the logs again. This seemed like the opportunity, and when my time was up I had no idea where my life would take me or when I would be back. "I just want to try to finish the logs," I sniffled.

"I told you not to make dreams with dates, but we can try," he said flatly.

I felt grateful that he stayed and worked with me on my worst days. That he mustered the energy and drive when I lost it. He climbed back up onto the tractor, and I guided him in the lifting of the log. We finally got it tacked into position after a full morning of struggle. I wondered if it would be better not to push through the off-times, but I knew if I quit when the going got tough, I'd spend the whole winter baking cookies or reading books. Every damn day brought a new reason to wait until later. I unlatched the log tongs, and Dad parked the tractor. We met at the tailgate of the truck. In silence, we fueled and oiled our saws, sharpened our chains, and moved to our respective logs.

I set my saw down, choked it, and pulled the cord. It stuck when I yanked on it, and I felt as if it had pulled my shoulder out of its socket. I yanked again and again, but the cord just kept catching. I couldn't believe that after all this time I still couldn't start my own chain saw. I just couldn't make the pull. I screamed and walked away from it, overwhelmed by the whole day. Dad finally set his saw down and came to show me how it was done. I stood back and watched as he bent over and made one fluid pull and the saw leapt to life. I went to kick him in the ass but he jumped out of the way, laughing like a big brother. I giggled and picked up my running saw, the chain whipping around its bar, and swung it at him. He grabbed his saw and swung back. We laughed hard enough to hear each other over the saws and through our earplugs. Then he stood there for a moment to monitor my cut.

Forest Husbands' idle clapped like a tambourine, flicking the chain around the bar even when I wasn't pulling the trigger. Full throttle was less a sound than a full-body experience. The rhythm snapped through my core as I followed the sacred blue line. Suddenly, the top of the nose hit the log, and it threw me back hard.

"Listen to that saw. It's talking to you all the time," Dad yelled over the engines. "Tools have their space just like a

partner in a dance. The space should be rigid and respected."
The saw was so heavy, it was easier to let it hang in front of
me, but I gripped my saw tighter and held my arms flexed.
"That's better," he said.

Near sundown, I could barely lift my saw into the back
of the truck. Dad grabbed the handle and helped me load
it. Quittin' time was almost an hour later than it had been
through the winter. Dad set his own saw in and grabbed the
ski poles that he liked to walk with, propping himself up
on the tailgate of the old, lifted Ford pickup. He had on his
Eskimo jacket with the hood up and his insulated overalls.
He dangled his feet off the back, took a look up at the sunny
west face of Mount Bachelor, and blew out a long breath of
blue smoke.

"Haven't been skiing much this winter."

"I know." I had bought a season pass to Mount Bachelor
and had been up maybe twice. I grew up skiing with my dad
most weekends, and was excited to have a winter with him
for the first time in a while.

"You should let yourself have fun, you know."

"This is fun for me." I meant what I said. I didn't have
any desire to go to the mountain. The two times I went were
because I felt guilty about the pass that I bought. "I'm content to build with you."

"Well good, but the next sunny powder day, I'm going
skiing."

I puttered around in the house, looking for tools in the
piles of sawdust. The sun gained momentum at that time
of year. It left the bottom of its cycle in December and
picked up speed sometime near the end of January. The air

had hovered around zero degrees with a mix of sunshine, gray clouds, and snow showers. I wore my fleece-lined wool beanie, three base layers, plus my canvas jacket, thermal underwear, oiled canvas pants, insulated gloves, and boots. I looked down at my body. It had taken on the color of my work: mud, grease, sawdust, hay.

Jumping out of the hole in the house that would be the front door, I turned west. The sun hung in the groove between the Middle and North Sisters and seemed to stall there for a moment. When I walked back over to Dad, the sun was sending that low, gold light straight into his eyes, lighting them from a flat brown to every color of the high desert. Juniper green, dry cheatgrass yellow, dark volcanic and sandy soils. He dropped his chin and brow into the glare. "Way to stick through the day, Sarah."

I nodded. It had been our sixty-third day without a break.

RESERVATION

After the first full week in April, the weekend came around. Mom and I rounded the ranch with a new horse in hand, familiarizing it with the hundred-acre pasture. New horses need to know the fence line so the herd or the wind doesn't push them through in the night, smooth wire slicing their hide.

"Where is the line?" I asked. "How close is it to my house?"

Mom meandered closer to the fence with horse in hand and stopped. "The property line is essentially right here along the fence." Then she held her arms out like the line was running through her from east to west.

I marched over to where she stood and whipped around. We were standing a couple hundred yards south of my house, not far beyond the log decks. I positioned myself on the line and moved from side to side so that I could see my house through the junipers, then walked up to the house and stared back at the spot where I had been standing. I marched up high on our property and looked back at the land. From there, I turned my eyes toward the other side of the valley, across hay fields, herds of Hereford cattle, and deer.

As I stepped off our property, I considered change. Bend, our nearest big town, was predicted to become the second-largest city in Oregon in the next ten years. It was forty miles away, but I knew how rich people liked to settle in the sage-brush where there's privacy and a view. It gives them a reason to drive their expensive cars. I considered the possibility of some kind of development across the property boundary. Would I be able to see it? Should I be planting trees now?

For the first twenty years of my life, my home at the end of Lower Bridge Road in central Oregon never changed. It's the kind of place that swallows a person's best efforts, which are truly only etchings in the earth, scratches that fill with dust and disappear. The first sign of change in the valley was nothing short of volcanic, a faux-French eyesore that erupted while I was in Africa. It stood out like another peak in the chain of Cascades on the western horizon. Perched on the edge of the rim over the ranch, the massive single-family home sat exactly fifty feet from our property line and thirteen feet higher than the legal standard. They dug their septic into solid rock.

When the notice had arrived that a family hoped to build on the edge of their 280 acres, and as close to us as pos-sible, my mom responded immediately with a whole list of economic and aesthetic reasons why they should not. She worried that a giant house that was built and potentially sold for a lot of money would cause the other properties in our area to be valued higher, so our taxes would go up. Otherwise, it's just a monstrosity that mars an otherwise pristine skyline. We didn't like it.

The court decided that because the giant house was not over a river and not technically "in" our view, the property owners would be allowed to go on with the construction of their dream home. I'd come to accept the new mountain as part of my life—the same way I accept the scar on my lip. They ran power through our property, and when Dad went to sign the paperwork, they told him that they couldn't afford to send their sons to college. Instead, they paved their driveway and left every light on. We watched them like fish in a fishbowl through the twelve giant windows in the front of their house. I never visited them and wasn't sure if I would be able to. They weren't neighbors. They were strangers. They built a gate, and I didn't even recognize their vehicles.

I walked the line again on the way back to the house, winding through the bitterbrush and desert lilies that were the first to emerge in the spring. The ground in front of me was awash in evening light, my shadow stretching east. I looked to my left the entire way, checking for any glimpse of my house. I felt suddenly paranoid about being closed in. I strode down to my parents' house, opened the back door, and the smell of fresh bread and steaks washed over me. Mom was leaning on the counter and turned as I walked in.

"She's right here."

I took the phone. "Hello."

"Ah, Sarah. This is Dougal."

"Nice day, huh? It's amazing how we go from mud to dust. Was there even one day of hard, moist ground?"

"Nope. Hey look, the neighbor to the south of me is making a Measure 37 claim to subdivide his land, and I was wondering if you could help me out. I've got a bunch of information to go through. I'd really like to let everyone in the neighborhood know about this. I think you only get a notice if your property adjoins his."

The zoning in our area had changed in the 1970s. The land had been sparsely populated, so there was no minimum for subdivision. As central Oregon filled up, the zoning changed so that rural land could not be divided into parcels smaller than 80 acres. Measure 37 essentially allowed people who bought their land before the '70s to make a claim to the county, and ultimately the state, for the land value they lost when the zoning changed. It was framed as a means to compensate a few people who could not provide a home site for their kids or were denied a building permit for a parcel that they bought years ago with the hope of retiring there. But the people making Measure 37 claims were using it as a vehicle to subdivide older family farms into housing developments and destination resorts. The county either had to pay the multi-million-dollar claims or grant the property owner the right to subdivide. People who had once been committed to their place had begun to look at their land like a cash cow.

Dougal and his wife, Katrina, bought twenty acres on the other side of Lower Bridge Road when I was a kid. I rode right through their place to get to the river. They lived in teepees and wall tents for years while they built a magnificent straw-bale home off the grid. Their place bordered a bit of public land managed by the Bureau of Land Management, but to the south and east lay a big ranch, seventeen hundred acres of farm ground that ran out to a rimrock on the edge of a sandy draw, a canyon where water runs in the spring-time. The draw felt as if it were as much mine as the land we owned. I grew up running my horse down the draw to the Deschutes River, just like the path I took with Nipper. We dodged badger holes, ducked junipers, blasted through herds of deer and coveys of quail, and always watched for mountain lions. I'd made the journey hundreds of times, first on my pony, then on my second pony, then on my horse. I kept tabs on the desert.

Mom and I arrived after dinner, and the fire in Dougal's woodstove flickered soft light onto the thick stucco walls of his house. We moved to a light in the kitchen and a pot of chamomile tea. Dougal greeted us with hugs. A slender, middle-aged man, originally from Wyoming, he had curly, dark gray hair and a smooth gait. He pulled out chairs for my mom and me and handed us each a mug.

"The reservation is closing in, but they can't make me go away." Dougal poured the tea and grabbed a folder from the local group of lawyers called the Central Oregon Land Watch. "We need to process this information and make a packet for our neighbors."

"Why haven't we heard about this before?" Mom asked as she added cold water to her tea.

"No one has—hardly anyone actually borders his land, and only contiguous lands get a notice from the county about development plans." He put on his glasses and shuffled through the papers. "I got the notice because we border his ground. I can see them digging septic test holes on the rim from my kitchen window."

I wasn't sure what to say. I thought back to just a few hours before and the overwhelming feeling I had of something closing in. I wasn't sure what it was. Maybe a single house on the empty dry-ground lot to the south of us. There are a lot of dry-ground parcels around, plots without water rights or farm deferral tax breaks. For my whole life, these parcels had been nothing more than bitterbrush, cheatgrass, and sage. Nobody's land, really: the kind of ground I rode my horse on to get to the public land along the river or the National Grasslands out toward Mount Jefferson.

When farming got tougher than ever and farmers were going broke, these parcels were sold off by farmers as building lots for the rich, who drove SUVs on the hourlong commute to Bend. Around the corner to the north and west, trophy homes overlooked a big, shallow pond filled with well water from the aquifer that the rest of us save for drinking. A little rowboat that no one ever used was pulled up on the bank.

When Dougal said his neighbors wanted to divide their whole place, I never expected it would be the arable land that would go. Farmland is the most expensive land to build on in the county. If the land's not farmed, the property taxes are insanely high. Generally, newcomers didn't want to farm and bought dryground outside our tiny irrigated valley, effectively leaving us farmers alone. Why would anybody want to live out there in the middle of a field that's either mud in winter or blowing dust in summer? It would take decades to grow trees big enough to slow down the wind.

Our irrigation district largely defined our community. My family and our neighbors owned the farmland within the greening reach of the district irrigation canal, in the Three Sisters Irrigation District. Once, in the midst of our community holiday party, the district's manager, Mark Thalaker, proposed that we all be deputized and put a toll on our single paved road that turned to dirt and dead-ended at Glen Cooper's place. Lafollette Butte, standing alone at the end of the McKenzie Canyon rim, formed the valley gate naturally. The back door would be where the road bends west and winds out of our farmland. The total area under our proposed jurisdiction was approximately eighteen square miles. We all hooted and hollered and raised our drinks.

Dougal lived on a piece of dryground and didn't farm. So Mom took a moment to explain our watershed and the issue with endangered fish. "Our water is diverted from the Wychuse Creek, which was historically home to steelhead trout," she said and set her tea down. "The people who implement the Endangered Species Act want to restore the spawning grounds at the top of the creek as part of a bigger project. First they have to create locks to allow the fish to migrate past the Pelton Dam on the Deschutes, and then our creek has to have enough water and be cold enough for the trout to come up and spawn. The water will come from farmers' water rights."

We had seen fractious farming communities to the north and south lose their water to fish. Historically, irrigation had priority, even to the point of sucking creeks dry by diverting their entire flow into irrigation canals. When endangered fish species took priority, communities lost their irrigation and watched their fields blow away. One woman left in a loaded old station wagon, a jar of soil on the passenger seat.

We knew the trickle of water left in our creek in midsummer—shallower than a fish was tall—wouldn't fly anymore. In 2005, the district received nine million dollars in funding to replace our canal with buried high-density polyethylene pipe. The majority of the pipe would be three feet in diameter and under extreme pressure as it wound down our valley. Our little canal would have to be dug into a fifteen-foot-deep ditch to receive the pipe, and the whole process was slated to take five years. The common goal was to conserve water for endangered trout species and to preserve irrigation water for our small family farms in a viable way. The hope was to fulfill the needs of both the fish and the farmers.

The five-year piping project started in the fall of 2006. A bunch of self-employed, self-broke farmers who had worked alone all summer were working together, all winter, for free. Other communities across the west that had decided to pipe their canals typically contracted the work out. My community decided to save four million dollars and provide the labor themselves. They started at the end of the road on Glen Cooper's place, working backward, from bottom to top. The bottom of the valley held the biggest farms with the most water rights, and consequently had the most at stake. Farms at the top of the valley had only minimal water rights and mostly enjoyed the canal flowing through their property like a spring creek. Replacing their pretty creek with a mound of dirt seemed like a rip-off, but the project was pushed legally by the Endangered Species Act, and we had to start construction. So Glen headed the charge. He was central to the piping project, both in building consensus in the community and running the welder. When Cooper showed up with the rest of the neighbors to release endangered steelhead fry into the creek, I knew the West was changing, and I was proud. They were out there in faith and rubber boots bending over the water to let tiny fry slip from their hands.

Now, sitting in the kitchen sipping tea, Dougal spoke about these water rights. "There is a rumor that my neighbor turned over five hundred acre-feet of his water rights so the new Thornburg Resort could go through." He shook his head. "His partner is the developer."

Mom flipped through law documents. "I used to know the Thornburgs."

I could see my mom's back reflected in the dark window behind her. She had her hair tied back and pulled her tea mug to her lips. "The Thornburgs leased that ground for grazing. They had no money. Their house burned down when they were in their eighties. They didn't have insurance, so they moved into their barn." One hot day in August, she and Dad were riding their horses out on the Thornburgs' land, grazing. She got so thirsty that she drank right out of the stock tank. When Mrs. Thornburg pulled up in the old water truck, she stepped out, bypassing "Hello," and said, "What do you think you're doing? I don't haul this water for a bunch of tourists to drink!"

Mom set her tea down now. "It's wild to think of a resort for rich tourists being named after that woman." Central Oregon was like that—a bunch of graveyards. New developments with three golf courses and six hundred homes preserved the names of what used to be there. Eagle Crest Estates, Deer Valley, River Run, Hawk's Nest, Forked Horn Ranchettes. Even Bend, the trendy recreation destination, used to be Bend in the River Ranch. There was an Angus

Acres too, but that's just funny. Gone are the family farms and open ground. All that's left are the names.

Even our farm, the old LBK, Lawrence-Blalock-Kibak Ranch, had been sold three times after my grandpa got too old to farm and the partners wanted out. Each partner got a dryground lot on the edge of the original property, back before I can remember. I've never considered the land my own, but I suddenly wondered if my blood was part of the original sellout. The old fields lay fallow and full of weeds, and they finally ended up in the hands of a speculator with a conditional use permit. The speculator kept a single-wide mobile home on the property to avoid repeating the permit process. Before Measure 37 went through, we lived in a zone of eighty-acre minimums, but after it passed I wondered if the old ranch would be the next gated neighborhood. Would they call it the LBK Golf Course and Resort?

By the end of the evening, we'd made a rough draft of a neighborhood alert letter for people to send in to the county and state Measure 37 Claims Units. We tried to think of why this kind of development should not be allowed in our valley. We scribbled down our reasons there in the soft light with another cup of tea. Mom and Dougal talked about property values, traffic, and wildlife corridors, the state's investment in our irrigation pipe, arrowheads and pictographs. With the growing demands for fuel and the focus on biofuels, we would need all tillable acres to provide for Oregon's fuel and food needs in the twenty-first century. My mind drifted into the deep reflections in the window.

I pictured the bend in the draw at the leaning juniper: I lean down and my horse's salty mane slaps my face. He jumps a giant piece of red rock and banks right. We pull out of the drainage before the badger holes. It's a short walk to the river's cliff edge from there. Pausing, we watch the wind on the water, and I know that the horse beneath me gives me everything I need to survive in the desert. The place facing subdivision is my favorite part of the world, a landscape that makes up my personal history. I've traveled it a million times, and the thought of it changing in any way sits like a weight on my chest.

My horse and I move on old, well-worn trails, like the wildlife that needs access to the river. In some places, where development spreads, a corridor is left for wildlife. Could I have a corridor? Would that be enough? Could I just continue life under new houses on the rim of my draw like I do under the house over the ranch? What would happen when all the rims were full? I knew I would be there longer than anyone else in the valley, and I was afraid of what I would witness. I was young, and I would live and die there. I planned to care for my parents so they could live out their days in the log house they built. I would be the next steward of our land, bringing up the fourth and fifth generations of that place. Was that enough to make me native? Who would save my habitat?

After our meeting with Dougal, I wrote to every newspaper in the state: "As an Oregonian, no matter where you live in this great state, you are seeing or will see the effects of Measure 37. The subdivision of our entire state is imminent. Our plan by default is sprawl, but we should not accept the default. Our responsibility did not end with the unfortunate passing of Measure 37. *This is a call to action, and it requires your vigilance.* As an active citizen, you can help to prevent the wholesale sellout of our farms and ranches. Protect your voice by writing to the county commissioner and state claims administrator about Measure 37 claims near your home. You can find claims in your area on your county's website under Measure 37 claims. If you don't write before a hearing, you will lose your chance to say something. Be at the hearings where the future of your neighborhood will be decided. Let your representative know how you feel."

I wrote to every Oregon representative: "I am the youngest person in my community, and I will outlive all of my neighbors who could potentially leave the valley in ruin with the help of Measure 37 as it stands. I am Oregon's youth, and I am pleading."

Most importantly, I wrote to the county and state to learn when the ranch claim across from Dougal would make it to court. I offered stamped and addressed envelopes for my neighbors to write, too. In the evenings, after working with the logs, I worked with Dougal to turn our community into a cohesive force with a clear vision of our future. I called to remind my neighbors when the hearings would be. I wished for even more hours in the day.

After nearly a quarter century of living in what seemed like an insulated, immutable valley, I was faced with real change. I couldn't help but wonder if there was anywhere I could retreat to. I'd been to a lot of places in the world, a lot of wonderfully remote places. Argentina? East Africa? But I continued to come to the same answer. No. No other place would do, not even the eighty acres next door. I had a place, a home. I had traveled so long and so far to be there, and it had become more than just where I could spend time with my dad. The place mattered to me, and with every day I couldn't imagine myself anywhere else. I was falling in love, but this was no river fling. That sense of vulnerability made me diligent.

After several weeks, I ran out of newspapers and representatives and neighbors. I didn't have anyone else to write to. I responded to the newspapers and representatives who wrote back, but gradually I let go. When it came down to it, I had no money, and money does what it wants. My parents own eighty acres, but for most of my life it had seemed like far more. Ultimately, those eighty acres would be ours no matter what, and that should be plenty of space.

I stood at the end of my driveway, looking up and down our imaginary toll road. I could see the massive home, mostly glass, perched on the rim, pressed up against the valley compound. There was irony in the conspicuousness of people who moved out here for privacy. That man-made mountain stood as a reminder of the community we tenuously protected with irrigation. I couldn't see my neighbors or their homes from where I stood, but I knew they were there, tucked into the folds of the valley as stewards of the land. I considered what it meant to belong to a community and a place. We were young and old, Republicans and Democrats, rednecks and artists, farmers and stoners, all gathered around a place. Together we were capable of change in order to stay where we belonged. And in the process, we became a community, over coffee and signatures in our kitchens. In every meeting we took time to talk about gophers and tractors and weather—never what it was doing "outside," as if the world were on its own out there, but about each man's, or girl's, task in it for the day.

MEASURING TIME IN TANKS OF GAS

By late April, after six months spent working the logs, Dad and I had finally developed a fluid process of moving raw logs from the deck to their notched and nestled position in the house. Other than being afraid, working with logs suited me just fine. I do not read directions or follow recipes. I was okay with what it took to make a square structure out of round material. I just finessed every single burl and bow. After months of cold, winter had lost the tangible weight it had had since November. I wore jeans instead of thermal layers under heavy oiled canvas, regular boots and cotton socks instead of clunky lined snow boots and wool socks. My head felt free under a light straw hat instead of encumbered by a fleece-lined wool hat, neck gator, goggles, and headphones. My hands felt nimble in thin pigskin instead of lined work gloves. God, the new season felt good.

We worked so hard, we measured time in tanks of gas. When Forest Husbands was out of gas, I set him on the bed of long white spirals of wood shavings. I put my earplugs in my pocket, lifted my goggles, and let the hot skin around my eyes breathe. Every time I refueled was exactly the same: I carried the saw to the tailgate of the truck and set it on its side, then dug in the white, five-gallon bucket for my saw tool. I levered the gas chamber open, then set the cap in a safe place where it wouldn't find its way to the dirt or wood chips. Pulling the funnel out of the bucket, I cleaned the end with my cracked forefinger before sliding it into the chamber. I shook the mixed gas and filled the saw to the brim. I put the cap on the gas and got ready to pour the bar oil in the other chamber. Dad taught me to fill it exactly, without any overflow. Oil moved sluggishly, so I had to stop when I saw the fluid on the upper slope of the tank. I pulled on my leather gloves to sharpen each tooth on the chain with a round file, so it would cut clean and straight. I put the jugs of fuel and bar oil, the saw tool, and the funnel back in the bucket and returned to my notch. Bending slowly to set the saw on the shavings, I lowered my goggles and replaced my earplugs. I loved not being able to hear with my earplugs in. I could shut the world out and just be in my own head. I didn't choke the warm saw. With a sharp half-pull from a curled arm and my left foot on the handle, I pulled it to life, picked it up, and refocused on the blue line.

I let the weight of the saw drop into the belly of the log. I was running it on a tilt about a quarter inch from the blue line. When the saw found a comfortable depth, I pulled it toward me and stepped back, slowly pulling the saw down the length of the log. Then I set the saw in against the other blue line on an opposite angle, carving out the V-groove. Again, I slowly inched backward, trying not to overwork the saw while its sharp teeth pulled long curls of wood out of the log's belly. When I got to the other end, I pulled the saw out and set it on the ground. Its chain bounded around the bar, snatching at the ground. I grabbed a crowbar and slammed the tip down into my cut and pried down. Then I moved a few inches and slammed the tip in again. I slammed and pried all the way down the log until long pieces like giant splinters came loose. I pulled them out and threw them to the side. I had succeeded in properly excavating the log, so I reached down to my thrashing saw and turned it off.

I left my earplugs in and goggles on, then leaned way back with my hands on my lower back, taking a moment to recover from being bent all morning. Sauntering around the other side of the house where Dad was working, I stepped into his view, and he took his finger off the trigger for a moment. I gave him a nod. He was running his saw upside down to leave a clean cut around the notch. Running a saw upside down cuts with a pushing chain instead of the pulling chain it cuts with when the saw is right side up. Usually a chain saw leaves a tattered edge, but by pushing the material away, the edge is left smooth. I wouldn't run Forest Husbands upside down because I was terrified by the way the saw recoiled when I hit the log wrong. I leaned back against the ancient tree to the west of the house and watched Dad work from the shade. I could feel the sun on my shins where the shade stopped.

He held his saw with one hand and bent down to paw the sawdust away with the other, inspecting the notch. He gave it a nod and a "that'll do" frown along with a shrug, then strolled around to the log I had excavated. I flicked the switch on the generator and strung the extension cord and grinder around to the log he had left. Dad took the wood to within an eighth of an inch of the blue line, and I took off that eighth with the grinder, splitting the blue exactly. Hard pieces of wood dust pelted my face below the protection of my goggles. I tightened my lips and held the whirling tool with both hands. With short blasts, I finished touching up the log. I turned off the tool and ran my gloved hand over the cuts. Whiffing the pine, I paused at the sunlight as it sifted through a tall juniper tree. My dusty amber goggles diffused the light in long rays, and I sat down to wait for Dad to tell me he had finished the other log.

The whine of the saw shut off, and I pulled my earplugs out. I could hear Dad take a long swig of water from the other side of the house. He stood still for a moment in the silence. I listened to him shift on the sawdust ground, picking up tools in one hand, the chisel, saw tool, and screwdriver clanking together. I heard him set his saw on the tailgate and move off to take a leak. I put my earplugs back in, flicked the switch on the grinder, and finished the log.

Once we had notched the logs we had on the ground, it was time to set them, take down the scribed logs, and tack new logs in position to be scribed. Dad checked the oil on the tractor while I amassed my tools for manipulating logs: sledgehammer, crowbar, hammer, chisel, and peevee for leverage to roll logs. I stapled long strips of fiberglass insulation into the V-groove, then flipped the log over for Dad to grab with the tongs. I waited by the log while he fired up the tractor. The sun felt warm through my sweatshirt, and the still air split suddenly when the tractor engine turned over.

Dad rolled around the back of the house and lined the tractor up perpendicular to the log. I fixed the log tongs to the center and moved to the light end, where I looped a rope around the log. I gave Dad a thumbs-up and held the log parallel with the ground by letting out the rope till the log hung a good eight feet over my head. Dad eased the tractor forward and lowered the log toward the wall. I levered the far notch onto its position, then guided my end into line with the rest of the stack. The log fit perfectly, and I thought to myself, "This is a first," but reveled in the moment while I shifted a ladder into position to clear the log tongs and the guide rope.

I gave Dad a nod, and he headed back to the log decks. I gathered some blocks and poles to tack up a new log, then ran to meet him at the next log that I had pointed out on our way up from breakfast. I cut a path down through the trees with Chyulu on my heels. My ankles twisted over the horse tracks in the mud, which had dried hard when the spring melt finished. We eased the log up the road to the east side of the house, Dad pausing while I tied the rope on the light end, then lifted it way up over my head. I hated the logs over my head and felt myself cringing. When the log hovered over its spot, I was in the wrong position, on the ground outside the house. I needed to be inside to tack the log down. If I let go of the stabilization rope, the log wanted to slip off its blocks. I stood there for a moment, unsure of what to do. I turned and tied the rope to the front of the tractor to stabilize the log momentarily. As I finished, I caught Dad's eye and saw him furrowing his brow at my idea, but he didn't say anything.

I jumped up into the house and tacked the log into position, nailing long poles from it down to the floor and out to the perpendicular walls. Standing back, it looked just right. I cleared the tongs, took my hat off, and waved it over the wall so Dad could see. He eased off the clutch while he looked behind him. Just as he pulled back to park the tractor for lunch, the log blew its stabilization boards. The rope was still on the log, which I had tied to the tractor for stabilization. It seemed like a flying death pin as it crashed down the east side of the house, shaking the entire structure. I sprinted up the ladder to see if Dad was okay. He was exploding in his little seat on the back of the old Farmall in his overalls and straw hat with his shirt off. "Fuck!" was all he could say. Ten times, with odd pauses between each exclamation. Each time I wondered what he would say next, but it was just another "fuck." It seemed to come from all over his body. His pores were wide open.

Finally, he came to a silence with the idling tractor. He looked up and said, "I haven't had a case of the fucks like that since I dropped an entire harrow-bed load of hay up at the barn." I remember that time. Mom came up from the house at a sprint and threatened him in such a way that he never exploded like that again, not where she could hear him, anyway. I laughed, and he got over it fast. We went through the entire process again, except for the tying-the-rope-to-the-tractor part.

Dad stepped off the tractor and climbed up into the window hole in the north wall. He was getting some elevation to see if the log we set was in line when the spring wind nearly blew him right out of the window. Maybe Dad didn't completely fall out the window, but I fell on the ground laughing while he held firmly to the wall with one hand and waved his other fist at nothing.

When we finished setting the log the second time, I had an impulse to rope the long nose of the tractor as Dad pulled away. I grabbed the rope, coiled it, and started running after the Farmall. Two swings and a full grab. Dad widened his eyes and pulled in his chin. He slowed down to let me take the loop off and slipped the tractor into fourth gear. He waited for me to coil the rope, then popped the clutch. Dad half laughed, half yelled over the engine, "It's hard to catch a Farmall 550!" The tractor lurched forward, and he took off like a madman, weaving down the driveway. He was raising and dropping the stinger with every weave. I chased him at a run, swinging my rope wildly. I made two throws, but no luck. He reached the log deck and parked for lunch, giggling and looking pleased with his ability to evade my efforts after that first easy nab. It became a ritual after that. We played.

As we strolled down for lunch, I looked out at my dwindling log decks. The logs were going up, and I expected to be excited to get through them. To live in the house was the goal. To light the stove and write and look out the window. But I was not at all looking forward to the end of the project, to the end of my time with my father. Log work was becoming my art and the house my studio, a space where only building happened; the building of a house and a relationship. He was giving me so much time and patience. He reached down into his bag and pulled out Chyulu's ball, giving it a chuck.

"Thanks, Dad," I said.

"For what?"

I smiled at Chyulu sprinting after the ball. "For everything."

Dad hadn't mentioned Mexico for quite some time. I knew I'd be leaving before long, but I allowed myself to pretend that I could stay forever—that maybe we could farm together. And when fall rolled around again, we could pick up where we left off and finish the house. The whole project felt like a great success.

FIRE AND TANGLED TREES

Our family knows how hard it is to build a house and how fast they can burn to the ground. The year I was in second grade, it didn't rain after the first of April. The ranch had run out of irrigation water by mid-July. The hay was short, but Dad cut it anyway and put it up beautifully green under those long hot suns. We were still living in the single-wide mobile home right beside where my parents worked on their own log house. It felt like living in a tin can in the desert. During the summer, we dripped with sweat at the dinner table. One summer night when I was eight years old—it was after midnight and too hot to sleep—I heard someone say the word "fire." We must have just had a lesson on house fires in school, because I have a vivid memory of grabbing my favorite blanket and bear, crouching down to smell for smoke, and carefully touching my door handle before opening it to the hall. I found Mom on the phone at the kitchen table, begging the fire department to come.

"I called an hour ago," she said, shaking her head. The outside corners of her eyes and mouth turned down. She hung up the old party-line phone. I felt a hot breeze on my bare skin from the open window to the west. Mom put her glasses on and looked up at me. Her brown hair fell forward over her naked white breasts. "Mamsy and Bompa's house is on fire, but everyone is okay."

I held my favorite blanket close and nodded.

"Put some clothes on, and we'll go down."

My grandparents lived about a hundred yards south of our house. The fire started at the power box in the garage. The aluminum wiring had shrunk, which exposed bare wire that grounded the meter base's framework. The ensuing spark was an unremitting white-hot electric flame, like a blowtorch with three leads. Dad said it looked like a medusa, but instead of stone, it left a pile of ash where the house had been.

By the time Mom and I arrived, two-thirds of the house was engulfed. Flames curled off the eaves and rolled upward, blasting into a spectacular peak fifty feet tall. My father stood at the base of it, emptying a red fire extinguisher into the heat. Its spray was so tiny, it looked like he was pissing on it. The two cars in the garage exploded, followed by a bunch of rifle ammunition inside the house. It was like what I imagine war sounds like.

The light of that fire was bright as midday. Once the house was fully engulfed in flames, it burned to the ground in ten minutes. The firemen from Cloverdale, a town about ten miles away, eventually came to watch. We live outside of the fire district, so the trucks come only to be sure there's no one stuck inside. The house had a sprinkler system, but the power to the pump went off when the fire started. Bompa stood at a distance with a meager pile of things. He held his Bible as the old juniper tree beside the house exploded into flames, long orange ribbons peeling up through its oil-laden limbs.

Never in my lifetime have I seen a fire in the juniper forest where I live, but that summer was so hot and dry, there was a lot of talk about the possibility of it. My usual job of helping to move hand lines and wheel lines for irrigation ended when the irrigation water ran out. The majority of the summer was spent pulling the dry weeds and brush around buildings and fence lines. We moved old woodpiles far from the house. The goal was to create a defensible area, which meant bare dirt with no way to carry fire.

From my house now, a sea of juniper trees unfurls in every direction, in subtle shades of green. They tend toward brown if they are laden with pollen. At just the right temperature and humidity in the spring they spontaneously explode into a cloud of pollen, sending the residents of the valley to their prescription allergy medications. In early fall they turn blue with berries. Mom makes Christmas wreaths out of them. Berries take two years to ripen, so there can be both ripe and unripe berries on the same tree. Rub the whitish, dusty bloom off the berry, and if it's ripe, it will be purple and taste sweet. Robins get drunk on the ones that fall to the ground, and then the birds come crashing into the kitchen window. I find them stunned or dead on the deck. The unripe berries are green and hard and do not taste particularly good. The trees' bark is thin, reddish-brown, and fibrous. The needles of the juniper are actually tiny scales, scratchy to the touch. Each scale has a small gland on its back where a bead of resin seals the pore to conserve moisture. The tree seems perfectly adapted to the high desert. Some people say it's too adapted, even invasive.

Juniperus occidentalis is our local variety. The old ones are beacons that have stood the test of changing seasons, climates, and land use year after year, some as old as a thousand years or more. They stand as tall as sixty feet. Today, however, the weathered grandfathers are surrounded by hoards of newcomers—during the past 130 years, juniper trees had spread at unprecedented rates. I knew this from the old aerial photographs that I saw at Pridey Holmes's place when we paid our annual mortgage. The Lower Bridge Valley was rolling grass, hardly speckled with juniper. The few buildings stood out with young poplars planted in rows, a hopeful wind and sun break for the future. Now, however, we were all tucked away in juniper thickets. The trees still around from the photograph were twisted and stately. The four that surrounded my house provided native shade that didn't need to be watered to survive. Thousands of short, scrappy junipers all growing on top of each other in every direction stopped at the edges of irrigated fields: too much water was the only thing that seemed to stop them.

Fire suppression and overgrazing had set the native juniper ahead and out of balance with the other native species, sagebrush and bunchgrasses. Its wide-reaching roots could extend more than forty feet from the tree, and its canopy could stop more than half of all precipitation from reaching the ground. The fibrous root system drew water to the tree and away from the rest of the high desert. Fire kept the juniper spread in check on shrub-grassland in the intermountain

West prior to European settlement. Fire occurred naturally on rangelands, and Native Americans used it to manipulate wildlife habitats. When settlers arrived, maybe even on the old wagon road that I can see in the ruts that cut through the hardpan behind my house, they brought livestock. Grazing reduced the fuel accumulations that played a significant role in natural fire regimes, and the juniper took over.

Juniper is an oily tree, prickly and twiggy, which makes it hard to render into much of anything, and only the toughest kids climb it. As a grade-schooler I climbed to the top of the biggest juniper in the geldings' pasture and swayed in the wind. I heaved on the slender end of the trunk fearlessly, but even if I had fallen, the dense limbs would have stopped me from hitting the ground, just like the rain. It burned well and smelled rich with sap, but most of the trunks are only four or five inches in diameter, not the kind of log that will burn through the night. People do build with them, mostly rustic furniture and picture frames, but the wood grows in a spiral pattern that continues to twist even after it has been cut and dried. I've seen a juniper picture frame twist right off a wall over time.

Despite how dry and fire-prone our valley seems to be, it hasn't burned for generations. Maybe the green fields keep fires in check. Instead, the pine forests on the rain-shadowed side of the Cascade Mountains burn every year. Sometimes torched forests burn again. Sometimes they're started by lightning strikes. Sometimes by arson. The smoke settles to the east. It rolls down through the rimrock funnels and lies over us like a brown blanket. The red sun is all that shines through, while the junipers eat up the smoke and stand tall year after year.

I remember the way that juniper burned next to my grand-parents' house. I remember their house reduced to ashes and the years it took to rebuild. I sit in my window opening, look-ing out at the juniper forest, wondering when it'll go ablaze. I imagine the charred landscape and that sour smell of rain on ash. But more importantly, I imagine defending my home. We are still outside the fire district, but with our new pipeline we would have pressurized water year-round for fire defense. I leaned my head against the logs and decided I would run a water line down from the irrigation mainline to my house for protection. With sudden conviction I turned to Chyulu and said, "We have to have a metal roof, no matter the cost." He lifted his head and gave me a blank stare. "Smart girl, huh? Thank you very much," I said, and when I smiled he teetered over on sleepy legs to be petted. As I laid my hand gently on his head, I thought, we'll be here for a long time together.

PURLIN

The log that runs through the center of the house and ties the entire structure together is called the purlin. I had been obsessing about my purlin log for six months, talking about it, walking by it every day, glancing at it, staring at it, and saving it, special. Occasionally I would squat down beside it and wrap my arms around the fat end. My fingers barely touched on the other side. Standing, I let my fingers drag over its worm-lines, knocking dust and mud to the ground. My purlin was the biggest log we used: a twenty-two-inch diameter, four notches, and an arch that looked beautiful and easy to do in the glossy pages of a log home magazine. In a moment of exasperation, Dad clamored over his quesadilla at lunch, "You'd have to be a fucking angel or have a helicopter to notch that bitch up in the air like you're askin' me to do."

"There's no time for your usual nap on the lawn today." I grabbed his plate and walked to the kitchen. "I'm leaving soon."

"Good," he said through a hearty laugh.

I left the dishes in the sink and we funneled through the mudroom, marching to what used to be the log decks. Now only one log remained. Dad stepped up the back of the tractor and swung into his seat, grabbing the glow-plug button, then turning the key. I stood at the log, ready, nervous. The engine turned over and labored into life. Dad let it warm up a minute before he inched forward and lowered the tongs. The front tires pressed into the dirt as the tractor labored to lift the log. I stepped to the end as Dad eased backward, turned, and headed to the north wall of the house. As we circled the structure I craned my neck to see it all at once, forgetting about my feet but keeping my hands on the butt of the log. The tractor stinger looked like a long snout since we had set it at full extension in order to set the final logs on the walls, which were now ten feet tall, on top of a three-foot foundation.

The massive log in my hands had to get to the middle of the house. It would have to span the east and west walls, then roll south to the center of the house from the north. Our problem was that both the east and west walls had giant window holes in them with only one log spanning the gaps. Those single logs seemed too puny to hold the purlin as it rolled. I imagined them screaming as they flexed under the purlin's weight, then suddenly snapped in half, the purlin crashing down.

"Where's the measuring tape?" Dad asked as he dug in his coat pocket.

"You had it last," I said as I kicked around in the piles of sawdust on the floor. Neither of us wore tool belts, and we were constantly looking for our tools. Dad said they pulled too much on his hips. And if he didn't use one, I wouldn't either.

"I've got it," he said, pulling the tape out. He measured the empty window holes top to bottom. "Forty-nine inches," he mumbled as he groped around in the sawdust for a scrap piece of two-by-six board. Pulling the tape down the board, he marked it at forty-nine inches, then picked up the Skilsaw. Holding the board over his knee, he zipped the end off, sending more sawdust into the piles on the floor. He set the saw down and held the board up to the window hole.

"Perfect, just a sixteenth too long," he said, handing the two-by-six to me with the tinted eye contact that happens through safety goggles. He picked up the saw and the tape and sidled to the other window hole. I slid the board in the hole at an angle, then smacked it with a hammer until it stood vertical, bracing the hole for the weight of the purlin.

When we'd finished bracing the other window, we headed back to the running tractor and the log. Dad climbed up the back of the tractor and plopped into his seat while I fixed my guide rope to the lighter end of the purlin. I took a deep breath and held it like I was dropping into a rapid, then gave Dad a nod. He eased down on the levers, and the log lifted slowly off the ground. I wrapped the friction-burned nylon rope around my hands, and as the log ascended I stood back, clenching my neck into my shoulders, letting the rope out. As Dad inched forward, the log started to swing and the chain links that held it cracked and squealed. Dad slammed the clutch in to stop the swing; he didn't take his eye off the log. Slowly, he lowered the log, and its ends found the east and west walls with a deep clunk. As the taut chain went slack, the log sagged down like a tightrope under heavy feet, and I wondered if it would snap in half under its own weight. We both paused, holding our breath, but the house cradled the log. I smiled, pleased that my house didn't collapse in that instant as I cleared the rope.

I stepped up into the roofless house and moved my ladder toward the purlin, approaching slowly, still scared that it might move suddenly, or that the little walls of my house would come apart under its weight. I wondered what it would sound like if all the logs suddenly fell apart, a deep rumble burying me in a pile of sticks. I climbed the ladder and grabbed the inside arm of the tongs. The rusted metal felt heavy in my hand as I jerked it away from the log and threw the tongs on the other side of the log so Dad could pull away. The tong had sunk an inch into the log like a giant fang. I poked my finger into the hole, tilting my head to see under the log. I tilted my head a little farther to see the stinger rising away from the log and the tongs swinging in the air as Dad backed up and parked the tractor.

I moved two ladders into place, one against the outside of each wall, so we could roll the log to the center of the house where it belonged. Dad climbed up the ladder on the west side, and I peered across at him as I balanced on the very top of the ladder on the east side. He wrapped his arms around the butt of the log and gave me a nod. As I levered it over, the log moved suddenly and my breath caught. What if it kept rolling, all the way across the house, and flew out into the air on the south side? But it came to rest, and I let my breath out, looking at Dad, whose eyes were wide. I levered the log again and it flexed in the center, its belly flopping down. I could feel that log up high in my back, between my shoulder blades, and down the sides of my neck. It felt like Class V whitewater.

It took us an hour to shift the log to the center of the house, moving the ladders after every ponderous roll. We blocked it up where I could scribe it and tacked it off with twice as many poles as any other log. Then Dad left me there to scribe while he readied the farm equipment for summer. He hung his goggles on a nail, picked up his bag, and loped down the gravel road. He wasn't leaving me in the lurch, just doing what was necessary. I needed to scribe it anyway before he could notch it up in the air, like an angel I guess, because a helicopter wasn't an option.

Chyulu stood by me in the doorway while we watched Dad round the corner at the end of the road. I turned around and looked up at the log. The scribing and notching would take forever, and I would be leaving in five days. I had come to find out, again and again, that the house did not handle deadlines well. Every task took three times longer than I expected it to. But this was it, the last log.

I had another river gig coming up and graduate school in Montana after that. I couldn't believe I was leaving again. You'd think that after working so hard to get home, I'd never leave—especially not for a river. But I was addicted, and it was the Grand Canyon that I was going back to. With a real home in my hip pocket—even half finished—I could leave. I was working toward a rare balance between wings and roots, a journey I had been on since my initial recognition of imbalance on the Tambopata. To have it all—a life that included time in one place for a home, community, garden, and maybe even a family. But a life that also allowed for re-creation and running free. I was looking for a way to lead a bunch of parallel lives, wrestle them together, tie them up, and call them a successful whole.

It was my dad who urged me to go, to keep rivers in my life better than he'd kept the sea. "You must be keenly aware of the need to vary your paradises, lest they become onerous, Sarah." He had paused in the doorway before he left and said, "Rest assured days will be where we get time to be together."

I smiled as he walked away, and I knew that the rest of the house would happen in small chunks when I had the time and money, but this had to get done. I stepped up the ladder with my scribe and studied the lines of the log. I tightened my focus from the structure to the log to the particular bumps in the log. The scribe line had to be precise for the purlin to sit down snugly. The finished placement of every log in the house had been a miracle. There was nothing standard, typical, predictable, or easy about any of them. But the purlin was the toughest. If my blue line wasn't accurate, the notching would be off and the log wouldn't fit. Neither Dad nor I could stand the thought of messing with that log up in the air if it wasn't perfect, and we certainly wouldn't be getting it back down to the ground.

Chyulu nestled himself in a pile of sawdust and looked up at me with his head resting on the ground. The way he pulled his eyes up scrunched his brow and made him look very worried. "You look pathetic," I told him. He didn't say anything back. I had an apple in a plastic bag that I took a bite from every hour until it was dark. Then I put a headlamp on and kept scribing. The blue LED light narrowed my focus on the levels of the scribe. The metal in my hands turned cold, so I put on my gloves and a sweatshirt. For a moment I looked out over the top of the walls into the juniper forest. The tips of every tree had moonlight on them. I blinked, took a deep breath, and kept scribing. At almost midnight, I rounded the end of the log where I had started. Taking the scribe off the log, I let my arms fall at ease. I stretched my neck and stepped down the ladder. Chyulu pulled his nose out from where he had tucked it and yawned. I reached my hand out to him as he wandered toward me, shaky on his legs. We walked home to my parents' dark house. Climbing the stairs to my room, I walked out of my clothes, leaving them on the floor, then crawled into bed with Chyulu. We curled up together and passed out.

The next morning Dad and I fed the horses and headed back to the house. I double-checked my scribing with Dad, who gave it a look and a nod. He was dreading the notching, because he would have to do it from the top of a ladder, climbing up and down with his chain saw. If the saw kicked, he'd fall or cut his leg off for sure. He stepped out to the tailgate and gathered his sharpened saw. I started it for him while he climbed the ladder, then handed the saw up, careful of the whipping chain. He didn't want me to work up there with Forest Husbands. My saw was too big and dangerous, so I stood at the ready with my earplugs in. And I stood there for nine hours, watching the saw blast him with wood chips. They rained to the ground while he carefully shuffled down the log, repositioning his feet and balance, cautiously cutting into the wood. I gassed up and sharpened Dad's saw, and he toiled over the notches. The sun drifted across the sky, throwing shadows, and I imagined the sun streaming through real glass windows.

At the end of the day, Dad had barely made it a third of the way down the log. His whole body ached from balancing up there, gripping his saw. We labored for two more days.

It was like he was sprinting at the end of the marathon. Dad was exhausted and I was impatient. We didn't talk much, just worked. And I was regretting it as it happened; we were losing the fun in our last days together. On the afternoon of the third day, Dad cut the engine on his saw and handed it down to me. We lifted our goggles and breathed for a moment. Without a word, I handed him the grinder, and he finished the log as best he could.

"There you go, beanpole," Dad said and climbed down. He threw an arm over my shoulder, and I leaned my head against him.

"Thank you so much, Dad. I could never have done this without you," I said, but didn't add that I wouldn't want to do this without him; that he was the whole point, and I cherished every moment he was willing to give me.

The log was ready to be tipped over into position. We moved our ladders to either end, then climbed in unison to the top of them. Our heads broke the skyline as we glanced across at each other. We stood there for a moment, up in the air, looking at each other in the impending moment of truth and possibly the end of an epic journey. I took a deep breath and started rocking that massive log, gaining momentum enough to tip it all the way over. "One. Two. Three." I said and sent it over. Dad threw his shoulder into his end and the purlin came over with a deep thump, then creaked down into position. I looked at Dad and gave him a shrug; then we stepped down where we could see the fit. We gathered under the arch where we could see the whole log. It was held off a full inch, leaving a gap between it and the log under it. I dropped my head, defeated. It could have been any of the four notches holding it off. Dad clenched his jaw in frustration, stepped out of the house, snatched his pipe out of his bag, and disappeared into the trees. When he returned, he said nothing. He fired up the tractor to lift one end of the log so we could excavate the notches. We cut and ground and chiseled, lifting and testing. The pink eventually went out of the sunset, and we could hear the horses nickering over the noise of the tractor. We were tired and cold, and the minute movements to set the log were too exasperating. The tractor finally choked on its own black smoke, and we decided to call it quits. Nighthawks swooped through the evening bugs. If it weren't for the whinnying of hungry horses, I'm sure we could have heard the gods snickering.

The big indigo dome of sky after sunset was perfectly clear, so we left our tools out and staggered home. I packed my car that night, ruminating over the log. I loaded my life jacket, bikinis, and sleeping bag. I had a day and a half before I had to head back to my other life, and as I packed I thought about my house and wondered why I was trying so hard to build something I might not even have time to live in. If I left after lunch the day after next, I would have exactly twenty-four hours to make the twenty-four-hour drive to the Grand Canyon to work a thirteen-day boat trip down the grumbling throat of the Colorado River. And that was what balance had come to look like in my life. I threw my bag in and slammed the car door, then turned and crumpled to the dusty, sunbaked ground beside it. I held my head in my hands and cried. I knew the house was a long-term project and I would return, but I wasn't ready to go. The purlin was the axis around which my future life would turn, and we'd made a half-assed job of it. Actually, we'd given it our very best effort and it wasn't good enough. I missed my dad already, his stories that took time, the squabbling over arches in the sunshine when we were both out of gas. Mom called out the back door that dinner was ready. I rubbed the tears away, stood, and walked to the door.

The purlin hung over me all night. In the morning, I sat down next to Dad at the breakfast table. It could have been any day, but it was the last full day. "I'm leaving tomorrow, and we *need* to finish this log," I said as I buttered my toast.

"I've got to finish sharpening the sickle bar on the swather. I start cutting next week, you know, and I haven't had a day off all winter, and I'm not going to have one all summer," he said, shoveling some eggs into his mouth.

"We can't leave it hanging up there."

"We can get back to it next season."

Next season, I thought, the log would be bleached and splintered, and I would have given my heart to one river after the next, farther from home every time. "But if that log isn't done, we won't be able to get a roof on, and the whole house will rot out in the weather."

Dad ignored me. He didn't care about time. He couldn't afford to. He could only take one day at a time, dealing with weather as it came. He would work until the job was done, even if that meant setting it aside for a whole season and coming back to it. And we couldn't see eye to eye on that.

We headed out the back door to feed the horses, like we did every morning. He was driving the truck while I fed half a ton of hay out the back for the horses on the dryground. I was trying to hurry the process, and Dad got pissed. He lurched the truck forward while I was bent over an open hay bale and threw me on my ass. I cussed at him, flipped him the bird, and left him there on the dryground with the horses half fed. I didn't look back, and I don't know what he did, but it felt an awful lot like Chile. I wondered if I'd grown up at all during that endless winter. It made me feel like a complete ass, and a failure to boot. I ran to my parents' house with Chyulu, tripping through the fence. I went straight to the paddock where my horse lived and I buried my face in his long black coat. "We're overwhelmed," I sniveled through tears. Nipper pressed his muzzle all over my body and hooked my shoulder with his jaw in a way that pulled me close to him, held by his neck. I thought about my dad and our respective realities. I was working with an impossible timeline and torn between two lives. Dad was looking summer in the face: fifteen-hour days, breakdowns, rain, heat, and dust. Nipper went back to eating, and I was sitting in his pasture when Dad pulled up after finishing the feeding by himself.

"Goddamnit," he yelled and kicked the truck. Chyulu lifted his head. "What do you want from me?"

I didn't respond. I just looked at the dry manure on the ground.

"I'm working as hard as I can!" he said and raked his fingernails over his face. I couldn't stand it. It's what he did when he couldn't cope. He'd rake his face till he bled.

"I know!" I screamed, "I love you. I'm sorry." My words blurted out through snot and tears and spit. He walked away, around behind the house, and I knelt down by the gate. All the love and trust and friendship we had built up over the past six months was crumbling. I didn't know what to say. I wanted to run after him, but I just pawed at the dirt while I wept.

Eventually I came to a sort of silence with choppy breath. I looked up with burning eyes. Dad was walking toward me. "The purlin is waiting," he said with a decisive nod of his chin. I pulled myself off the ground, gave Chyulu a stroke down his back, and followed Dad up to the house. The sun shone bright on the green blanket of the desert in springtime, and I felt an overwhelming sense of grace. We set ourselves to fitting that log all afternoon, in silence, and even at the end of the day the purlin wouldn't set down. Dad fired up the truck and backed down the road. I closed the wire gate behind him and got in the passenger seat. I had never wanted so much for time to slow down.

"Tomorrow is your last morning?" he asked, letting the truck roll slowly through the pasture.

"Yeah," I said and hung my head.

"We can try to start early and see if we can get that thing to set down."

"Thanks, Dad. I'm sorry about all of this. I'm sorry about the end of time and how it takes the fun out of everything. I'm sorry for asking so much."

He shut the truck off behind the house. "You're fine, Sarah," he said.

In the morning, we did start early. As we topped the rise on the way to my house, where we could see the farthest east, Dad and I stopped to watch the sun drench our valley. The air was crisp against my face, and the desert felt humid for that moment in the morning when the sun hits dew. "I want you to know I am proud of your efforts as a person," he said after a long silence. I took the praise quietly. Unless you spend seasons on a dusty, muddy, desert ranch with hungry mouths, busted fence, and broken-down equipment, your opinion doesn't mean a damn thing to him. There hadn't been a day in a long time that he hadn't seen me right there beside him. My hands were cracked just like his. I packed around the same heavy canvas on my back all winter. My back hurt, and I understood his pace. After pushing that pace all winter, I knew why it was important to slow down. He told me I worked harder than three men put together. It was at once a compliment and a criticism. Yeah, I was tough, but I hadn't truly learned that a person could work herself to death out there, and he let me know it.

We set to minute excavations on the purlin. I craned under the arch as sawdust from the grinder blasted me in the face. The whine of it was higher pitched than my chain saw, piercing through my earplugs. Dad sat quietly on the tractor with his hand on the levers. He moved the log up and down while I ground and tested. At noon, I motioned for Dad to set the log down, then flipped the switch on the grinder. I was flat out of time, but the log sat down well enough. It wasn't the tightest fit in the house, but it would hold the structure together. Dad and I stood back and gazed at it, the sun warming our backs.

"Thanks, Dad," I said, reaching out for his hand.

"You're welcome," he said, and squeezed my hand.

DESERT HIGHWAYS

Austere scenes flashed by as I rolled south into Monument Valley. My left leg was out the open window. A skinny dog shat under a Mustang Gasoline sign. As if in a snapshot, I watched the dog get blown over by a gust of wind and dust. He struggled to catch himself, and then I was past. The late-afternoon shadow of a butte stretched across the road from a mile away. The highway bent right, and I took my foot off the gas as I passed a dead horse that lay stiff-legged against a barbed-wire fence—white bones except for some leftover sorrel hair on its face and hip. The ravens were done with it. I found them a mile later, pecking at a small carcass ground into the pavement.

The sun slipped below the horizon, and I turned on my headlights. I passed the first vehicle I had seen in an hour, a big black truck filled with big, dark Indians. Neil Young was playing "Harvest Moon" on the radio, and my gas showed

I had less than a quarter tank. The next town was a long way out, so I let my foot off the gas a little and dropped my speed to seventy-five miles per hour. I was thinking about the Colorado watershed. About running an entire river.

It had been a month since I'd left my folks at the ranch. I had run several sections of the Green River and was on my way to run the Grand Canyon again and after that the upper Colorado through Westwater and Cataract canyons. Eleven hundred miles downstream, my life felt like one long highway, sometimes asphalt, sometimes muddy water sweeping around cliffed bends. Either way, the deserts of the Colorado Plateau unfolded in every direction. I leaned my head against the headrest and wiggled my toes. I was home, yet so far from home. I reached for my cell phone on the passenger seat and checked for bars. No reception—typical. I turned up the music and stared down the highway into the night, wondering why I was headed south. I fought my house and my dad and Chyulu out of my head.

Eventually I rolled into a sleepy town and ducked into a gas station. I fumbled around for my flip-flops in the pile of crap in the backseat. I put a T-shirt on over my bikini top, popped the gas flap, and stepped out of the car. I suddenly felt light-headed, and I held on to the roof of the car. When my vision cleared, I glanced at the price of gas. Well over three bucks. I sighed and started the pump.

I wandered into the Quickie Mart for an energy drink and found an old Navajo couple at the fountain drink machine, each filling a vast, insulated vessel labeled *Immerse Your Thirst* with Cherry Pepsi. I complimented the woman on her turquoise jewelry, paid, and wandered back to my car.

As I eased back onto the highway, the moon rose full over a mesa to the east. I cracked my energy drink and glanced at the clock. Two in the morning. I would be rigging my next trip at eight. If I didn't stop again, I might get an hour of sleep.

The yellow dotted lines pelted the front of my car, and I drifted through the silver desert, lit by the moon. It was odd to be up high, where I could see into the distance, after so many weeks in deep canyons. I always suffered from a vague claustrophobia on the river, and I realized it only when I emerged onto the rim where I could actually see. The recognition of distance let home slip back into my thoughts. I riffled blindly through the stuff on my backseat as I drove, looking for a pen and paper. I pulled them out and began to write one word at a time while I drove, glancing up at the yellow line to keep the car on the road. I wrote about my home ground in silver light, the nights I ran my horse to the river over the white sand or white snow. When I stopped at daylight to take a piss, my story was dappled by teardrops, blurring the ink.

BURIED

In the high desert, water is fickle. When surface water comes, it arrives in torrents of rain and snowmelt. Ground water is sneaky. When people drill wells, many attempts come up dry, and the ones that produce water pull from at least three hundred feet below the ground. But then springs flow into the Deschutes, doubling its size in ten miles. I can remember a shallow well with a cap on it next to the first house my parents lived in. Mom would take me out there on hot summer days and lift the cap off. It sounded like a river flowing in there, and cold air rushed up into my face. Most people's wells didn't tap into those underground rivers, and in dry years they went broke trying to farm, because farming depended on snowpack. The amount of snow in the mountains meant a lot to farmers. Jawing about weather in the middle of Lower Bridge Road, they didn't sound much different than powder-hound skiers.

But what was more important was when the snowpack melted. Water for farmers was diverted from Wychuse Creek into a canal system for irrigation. The creek itself dropped into a deep ravine of stinging nettles and ticks. An early melt from rain on snow in the mountains would whip water down into the creek and away, because our irrigation district had virtually no storage capacity. Farmers could run water into irrigation ponds, but only enough for a couple of days of irrigation—not enough for a season.

As a kid, I spent summers at the big old LBK irrigation pond. The water flowed into the football field–size pond on the west end and was pumped to the field from the east. The east end was also the deep end, where I could sink ten feet down to where the water hadn't been warmed by the sun. I sat cross-legged, holding my breath in the cool water. My cousins and I played endlessly there when they visited in the summer. We harassed frogs, slung mud, and played with Dad's sailboard in the gentle breezes that rolled over the water. Grown and showing up again at the ranch at the end of August after my river life had eaten up another summer, Nipper and I rode by the pond. My body rocked with his long strides, his back felt warm between my legs, and I let my feet dangle, bobbing without stirrups. Nipper's hooves slipped down into the fine mud along the bank as we wandered toward the old juniper tree. I scanned the ground absentmindedly, looking for arrowheads amid the sagebrush. I bent down as we walked under the tree. All that was left of my childhood empire were a few bits of brittle plastic from the chairs where my aunt and Gramma used to sit for hours while we played.

I had a couple of weeks to put into my house before I had to leave for graduate school in Montana. I had decided to pursue environmental science and writing, even though I knew I just wanted to take over the ranch. I don't know why I felt the need to pursue something that I might well not need. Maybe because people told me education was important, but—and this is a common predicament for a young person taking over a parent's business—education isn't enough.

Dad was in the middle of haying. I set to oiling my logs so they wouldn't rot before I could get the roof on. Temperatures hovered in the high nineties from about eight in the morning to eight at night. I circled my house, following the shade. Midday, we had to cool off to make it through the afternoon. I set down my oily paintbrush, wiped my hands on a rag, and left the house with a bikini in my back pocket. I was headed up to meet Dad at the irrigation canal that flows through our property at the base of the rimrock. I called for Chyulu, who had passed out under a tree. He shook his head and caught up with me through the juniper trees. Dad drove the red truck from the fields at the end of the road. In the back of the old Chevy with the tools, fluids, parts, wire, and twine lay an old white-and-blue surfboard that Dad had brought home from La Jolla a couple of decades before. On the automatic gearshift hung a pair of little blue Speedos.

I arrived a few minutes before him to change behind a bitterbrush. I pulled my surfboard out from under the branches where I hid it, then sat on the grassy bank of the canal, flicking the quick black ants off my toes. Chyulu poked around in some sagebrush, then lay down beside me. I scratched his stomach. The water wasn't milky from snowmelt that late in the season, but it was plenty cold. The canal was only about five feet wide and two feet deep, flowing steadily through willows and alder. It wasn't much, but it was enough.

I turned to watch Dad cross our smaller ditch, which we'd diverted from the main canal for our irrigation. Stepping along the plank at the headgate, he climbed over the barbed wire fence wearing his everyday uniform of blue overalls and boots, shirtless under a wide-brimmed straw hat. He set his board down beside mine and then disappeared behind a bush to change and smoke. I stepped down into the water with my board to get a head start. Pushing my board in front of me, I laid my belly down into the cold water and started paddling, fast and tense. Upstream I glided, careful not to plunge my cupped hands more than a few inches down, or I might take off a fingernail on a rock.

I ducked under the willows and alders that hung over the water, soothed by the green banks at that dusty brown time of year. Before long, Dad caught up with me and tried to pass. I tried to paddle as fast as he did, but he passed on the right, his silver hair slicked back. I grabbed at his feet and squealed, but he made it by. He was headed to his only relief in summer.

About a half mile up the canal, the water dropped over a little ledge and curled into a wave, maybe a foot tall. Dad had rigged a rope from a willow tree that he could hold on to while he plunged into the white bubbles, holding his breath for as long as a minute. As I rounded the last bend in the canal, Dad was setting his surfboard on the bank. He tugged up his sagging Speedos and stepped toward his desert wave, grabbing the rope that he left neatly looped in the willow, standing there for a moment as the quick water moved around his legs.

I stepped off my board and set it on the bank, then sat down slowly into the short, bristly grass. From there I watched Dad's ritual, as I had almost every hot summer day growing up. Chyulu bounded out of the water, slinging droplets from his tail. Dad gripped a rope he had tied with one hand on either side of the canal and let himself down into a push-up position. He faced upstream, his head just barely out of the water. He paused and took a breath, then submerged himself into the wave. He weaved back and forth like a fish swimming upstream, while the clear water streamed through his silver hair and down his dark auburn back. I wondered how many coastlines flashed before him— New Zealand, Costa Rica, Hawaii, La Jolla, the Dominican Republic. The aerated water became teal blue. Maybe he was waiting for a tropical fish to come careening down the canal, as out of place as he was. Or maybe in his mind's eye he had paddled out through a huge ocean swell and was now diving under a breaking wave, waiting for it to roll over him so he could come up on the other side, in position to catch a big one, all the way back to a white-sand beach.

Eventually he lifted his head out of the canal. The freshwater evaporated immediately in the desert breeze, and he let me have my turn. I usually liked to be in a boat, so plunging into the wave only brought back memories of long, deep swims in rapids when I should have kept my boat upright. I came up sputtering, clearing my nose and ears. I sat back in the grass next to Dad, and we relished the fresh feeling of cold water, washed clean for a moment of the heat and dirt and sweat and desert.

"I know the piping project is the only way, but I don't know what I'm going to do without this water," Dad said as he stretched his toes in the water.

"I'll miss it too," I said, thinking back to the winter before, when we'd signed the plans to replace our canal with a pipeline. There had been talk of piping the canal for twenty-eight years, because of the drop in elevation in the valley and the advantages of pressurized water. When farming communities in Klamath Falls and along Mill Creek began to lose their water to endangered species of fish, a piping proposal came to the fore in our irrigation district. Historically, our creek had been home to endangered steelhead trout. For a hundred years, we had diverted water from Wychuse Creek to an irrigation canal that lost almost half the water to seepage and evaporation.

After Klamath and Mill Creek lost their battles, our irrigation district manager, Mark Thalacker, saw the writing on the wall. Farmers would no longer take priority over endangered fish. The time was just right for funding and for getting farmers to sign on to a piping project. He focused on the benefits of pressurized water to get the farmers on board, while fish remained in the background, like a storm cloud on a distant horizon. In 2006, when the Fish and Wildlife Service decided to reintroduce the endangered steelhead into Wychuse Creek, our piping plans kicked into high gear. The creek was no longer a "historical" spawning ground; it was clearly and immediately *the* spawning ground of steelhead.

Farmers met in small groups for two years before coming up with a plan for all the landholders along the irrigation canal to sign. Funding agencies would not get behind the project if there was any significant dissent in the community. On the other hand, if our community could not decide on a collaborative solution, the Endangered Species Act would provide the Fish and Wildlife Service with the power to put water back in Wychuse Creek by whatever means necessary. Either way, our irrigation canal had to go.

The winter before, I had stood at the back of the final Squaw Creek district meeting with Dad, waiting to sign the final draft of the piping proposal. We had finished work on the house for the day and had fed the horses before driving the old Chevy to the district office for the meeting. Sixty folks in folding chairs lined the room; every single one of them lived on the canal and would be affected by the pipeline. Every single one of them had to sign the plan for the district to get the $10 million in funding to build it.

In front of the crowd sat the three water district board members. Karen seemed small sitting between the two old men—a sparrow perched between two turkeys—but she was outspoken on the edge of her chair, leading the meeting. It was the women I heard, opinionated women. The meeting ran like a greased machine among Karen and the wives. I hadn't heard a man's voice in two hours. They moved through the legal agreement for the piping project, Karen reading every word of six single-spaced pages aloud. Essentially, as a community we would bury our water in a high-density polyethylene pipe that would follow the same course as the present canal. It would travel eighteen miles through many small private lots with no historic right to the water, down the valley to the fifteen or so big water-rights holders. There was nothing new about this, except that the riparian ribbon the canal created would be replaced by a mound of dirt. We could get the $10 million from various agencies if we provided the labor as a community—this was called "in-kind." Essentially, we had to do the pipeline project ourselves. Our time and equipment and sand were all worth something, and that's how Mark Thalacker could keep the money coming.

When Karen finished reading, she looked up and asked if there was any opposition. Only one woman raised her hand. She owned a small parcel at the top of the district that our canal flowed through. She didn't own any water rights, but she liked the canal. It was her seasonal creek, where willows and ponderosas grew in an otherwise dusty place. She didn't want to lose her creek to the pipeline. I understood how she felt, but she was the only one to oppose the plan. As sincere as the call was for opposition, opposition wasn't an option. If we couldn't decide on a plan to keep our water, then the Fish and Wildlife Service would take the water away with the power of the Endangered Species Act. Either the canal would be dry or it would be a mound of dirt with a pipeline under it—either way, the riparian ribbon would be gone.

The landowner spoke passionately about her canal, her tone alternately sad and reproachful, as if it were the farmers' fault. The accusations hurt our feelings, because we felt as sad as anyone to see the canal go. I turned to Dad, who looked stricken. I wondered if he would suddenly throw his hand up and back the woman. His desert wave would be gone, and there would be nothing to soothe his desperate longing for the sea. But he kept his hand down, and I reached over and held it in my own. My mom and Mark tried to be as sensitive as possible with the canal lover. Mom did most of the talking while Mark shut up the farmers in the back of the room who were saying things like, "It's been a long time since we had a fire in the upper canyon." That one landowner refused to sign, so we amended the plan to start the project backward, at the bottom end of the canyon, where the farmers were ready to go. People mingled afterward and waited to sign. Dad and I moved up to the table and hesitated; then we both signed on, bidding farewell to our ribbon of relief through the desert. There was no disputing that the endangered fish needed water. Dad turned to me and said, "We're going to restore the fisheries so we can eat trout when we get put out of the farming business."

When the pipeline started that winter, we volunteered just like we'd signed on to do. Several miles of ditch got dug, then pipe got welded and buried, but the project hadn't made it to our place yet. Now it was summer again, and Dad and I were enjoying our last summer of the canal. Chyulu lay down next to Dad, who reached out and pulled gently on his ear. Dad was still wiggling his toes in the water when he said, "They're going to have me back workin' on the dang pipeline as soon as I'm done farming. Maybe even before." Dad hated the pipeline ditch. "I hate holding the stick for the guy in the excavator so he could keep the digging on grade. That constant impact of steel on the earth gets into my brain and my body. It jars me," he said. But more than anything, working on the pipeline was like suffocating his best friend. The canal provided his only respite in the maelstrom of farming. Now the water would tear on by, underground and under pressure.

"I'll put in some time this winter for us," I said as I picked at a willow leaf.

"That'd be nice," he said as we lay back down on our boards and floated easily downstream. Dad changed back into his overalls, loaded his board, and headed back to the field. I stashed my surfboard and walked back to my oil can and paintbrush for the afternoon. We would meet again at the dinner table after dark, around ten in the evening that time of year. Mom made a full meal from scratch no matter what. Sometimes we sat down to dinner after eleven, just to get up and eat again at five in the morning.

Volunteering on the pipeline was just a different kind of community service. We weren't baking cookies, landscaping an old folks' home, or decorating Christmas trees for hospice. I was home for the holidays from school in Montana the winter after I told Dad I would help on the pipeline. I called to let Mark know I'd be happy to help, and he was eager to have me. He picked me up the next morning at daylight.

"I've got you helping Glen with the welder and driving the track hoe this week," Mark spoke up over the hard rock on his radio.

"The track hoe?"

"The excavator. I refer to her affectionately as Godzilla," he said and smiled.

I wondered what exactly I was getting myself into. I'd driven some equipment growing up, mostly tractors. We headed to Glen Cooper's place. Here, it's not a farm or a ranch or a house or land. It's a place. Cooper's place, Kitsen's place, Simpson's place, Lawrence's place. Mark dropped me off and headed to the office. "I've got to keep finding the money," he said as he sped away in his white Jeep Wrangler. I walked into Glen's house and Charlene, whom we all called Red, made me some coffee, which I don't drink. We talked about her health problems, and she gave me some old Halloween candy.

As I followed Glen out the door to his old white Ford, Red yelled after me, "He's a horse's ass to work with."

I turned around, caught slightly off guard and amused.

"Just walk away if he's doin' somethin' you don't like."

I grinned and nodded. There were stories I'd heard over the years from neighbors. One time Glen sent his wife across a steep slope on the tractor and it ended up rolling on top of her. Another time he dropped an entire building on his son. They were moving an old barn, and Glen assumed Louis was out of the way. Both survived, but Glen had become notorious.

"I walked home all the way from the field the other day when he set the dynamite off while I was in the hole," Red squawked.

I gave an uneasy laugh and got into the truck. I'd known Glen all my life. When I was little, my mom used to call Glen to let him know I would be over to trick or treat. He always gave me the whole bag of candy, since there weren't any other kids in the neighborhood. This was the first time I had worked with him. We bounced up the pipeline road and pulled up to a backhoe with a set of loading forks tipped over in the mud beside it. Glen stepped out of the truck without saying anything. He walked to the hoe and fired it up. Lining up with the forks, he yelled at me to hook them up with a chain. My fingers weren't nimble in my big insulated gloves, and I was slow to attach the chain. I guess he thought I had taken long enough, so he jerked the bucket up and nearly pinched off two of my fingers between the chain links.

I gathered myself and walked back to the cab, looked him in the eye through his thick square glasses, and said, "Don't ever move a piece of equipment around me unless you can see that my whole body is out of the way."

Glen sat back in his seat, startled that the little girl before him would say such a thing, but he didn't make me nervous for the rest of the time we worked together. Later we traded places; I worked the equipment and he worked on the ground. I was far more careful than he could conceive of being, and he put himself in positions that I never would, so we worked well together.

We were working with polyethylene pipe that was three feet in diameter and three inches thick. Mark chose to spend the money we'd received on new technology that could potentially last a thousand years rather than PVC pipe, which starts to break down and fail after thirty years. Mark didn't have kids, but he cared about what would happen in my lifetime and the lifetime of my kids. He didn't want to be repairing the pipe when he should be retired. He believed in the lifestyle of the small family farm, and he was set to preserve the ones in our valley.

The pipe was heavy. At one point the weight of it pulled Glen, the backhoe, and the $130,000 welder sliding toward the ditch even though Glen was standing on the brake. At the moment Glen realized there was no stopping the pull of the pipe, he slammed the hydraulic levers, sending his digging claw in an arc out the back of the hoe. It rammed into a ball of mud, dirt, and rock. Clutching for purchase, it caught just before he dropped off the edge of the fifteen-foot ditch. He paused momentarily in the aftermath of a near miss, then set his hand on the levers. Easing them down, he used the digging claw like a winch to pull him, the pipe, and the welder back up. I must have screamed, because after he pulled himself back, he turned down the RPM and said firmly, "Don't panic."

"There wasn't anything else I could do," I stammered, thinking to myself that I didn't believe a seventy-three-year-old man could move that fast.

A few neighbors volunteered faithfully on the project. Every morning, Mark told us when to show up, gave us a briefing, and then left for his office. At the beginning of the week, Chuck Mo excavated the ditch with Godzilla. He had about thirty years of experience, and the ditch was always perfectly on grade and uniform, the dirt set tidily to the side for backfill. Meanwhile, Glen, with the help of Kelley or me, welded fifty-three-foot sticks of the pipe into thousand-foot sections in the Long Hollow field where he had plenty of room to move it around. Once the week's worth of ditch was dug, we dragged the big sections of pipe down along the ditch. For the second half of the week we welded the long sections into the project, dropped them in, bedded the ditch with sand and then back-filled. This was about the way our process went and would go for five winters.

I loved the project, and I loved my neighbors. I felt like a little boy—giddy on the giant equipment. Dad was glad not to be on the ditch—instead he sculpted in his shop. But he wasn't happy. He was talking more and more about Mexico and his blue board. When I got home from working on the pipeline, I listened to him talk about the sea.

"You should go, Dad, just like I have to go to the river. I'll be here. I'll cover for you."

He thought about it for a second, slightly baffled that the talk could become reality if he really wanted it to. "But what about your mother and all the horses?"

"Well, I'll be here for two months between semesters. I'll feed, work the pipe, and Mom will be fine." He looked me right in the eye and waited for me to go on. "It's hard to leave, Dad—gut-wrenching, really. I am often homesick the entire time I'm gone. But I know I have to go, and it might be the only way for you to find peace, with this place and the sea. I think the closest thing I've found to balance is making myself leave so I can come home."

Dad didn't say anything, and I left him there. I knew he was thinking about it. Acting on all he had said over the years would be different than talking about it. Not to mention, the sea had denied him every time he'd tried to go back.

My second day on the project, I ran Godzilla. Four main levers moved in several directions to operate the bucket, arm, and tracks. The machine was sensitive and I was gentle, so the men let me stay, situating the ends of the long sections of pipe into the welder. I manipulated the pipe with Godzilla, and Kelley built me a road with the Caterpillar dozer wherever I needed to go. We definitely tore up the ground. It was a narrow strip, but that disturbed ground would be covered in weeds come spring.

We didn't have a foreman. No one was in charge. No one seemed to know exactly what was going on. But we sure laid a lot of pipe. I moved the track hoe where common sense told me it should go, and no one ever told me otherwise. I spent a lot of time sitting on Godzilla, holding the pipe for the welder. I had to monitor the hydraulics to hold the pipe steady. If it sagged, the weld would be compromised and would result in a geyser come summer. I sat there with my earplugs in, feeling the rumble of the machine in my body, recalling what Dad had said about Godzilla. "It's an abrasive mechanical experience. The steel striking the ground seats in your mind."

When five o'clock rolled around, I realized I had been on the project since eight and we hadn't eaten anything. These men didn't take breaks. We worked until we were done and then we went home. Just before we got in our trucks, we watched the sun set behind the Sisters. A blue heron flew through our field of vision.

"There goes that blue heron I see every day about this time," Glen said. He turned to Kelley. "He's headed to your pond to go fishing."

"At least we'll still have our ponds, even when the pipe is done," Kelley said, smiling.

I felt like we were part of something intricate, where humans and animals interacted like familiar neighbors. At the end of it all, there would be a little water for everyone. Everyone except Dad.

BOUND ENGINE

Forest Husbands died after I went back to Montana. The first sign of ill health was when it got harder to pull him to life. My short-jerk trick wasn't working; it felt like the engine was seized. I kept his fuel and bar oil tanks full, the chain sharp, and the poor old guy stayed in the mudroom at night where it was warm.

Dad had spent that fall rendering my leftover logs into firewood. He used Forest because he was more powerful than the old Stihl, which was made for the more refined art of notching. At twenty-two pounds and 8.4 horsepower, Forest sits in Dad's shed now, his engine bound. When the Husqvarna repair guy told me the fuel hadn't been mixed right, I couldn't speak. I felt like I'd foundered my good horse or poisoned my dog.

Dad and I had a ritual at the tailgate of our old red truck with the five-gallon buckets full of gas and oil and saw tools. Dad taught me to take great care in mixing my fuel and keeping it clean, to shake it every time before I added it to Forest's tank. Mom said maybe the damage was done before we got the saw. I suppose this is a possibility, but I don't know why it would have taken so long for the engine to become paralyzed. Judging time in tanks of gas, I'd say I ran Forest for hundreds of hours. I wonder how many trees Forest felled before he came to me. I wonder how big they were. I imagined him leveling a forest in the hands of a modern-day Paul Bunyan. And now he was dead.

My chain saw dying just topped off the anxiety I'd felt in Missoula that made me pull my eyelashes out. The city lay under a smothering brown blanket of inversion, and the constant odor from the cardboard plant twinged in my dry, cracked nostrils. Montana was heavy on my body. I thought maybe I had seasonal depression, so I went to the full spectrum lights of the tanning tubes. I snuck in there, embarrassed to be seen by anyone, and fell asleep under fluorescent lights that did nothing for me. I missed the ranch and my parents so badly, even though school was fairly engaging. Leaving the place for the river was one thing, but for some school in a shitty town was another. I'd get through the days all right, but I'd disintegrate at night. I sank into Chyulu's bed and wept with my arms around him until I fell asleep.

After my evening seminar class, when my classmates headed to Flippers, a local smoky bar, I usually went home. I preferred to be alone. One night, though, I went on over to Flippers. I don't know what got into me. My ride was going and said we wouldn't stay longer than one beer. We pulled extra stools around a table and sat with several pitchers of Kokanie between us. Some folks lit up American Spirits while ex-smokers enjoyed them secondhand. It must have been the way I carried myself, or my face, because a guy I knew suddenly said, "Place doesn't matter, Sarah. You need to be content with yourself." I didn't know where this guy was from, but he'd lived in Montana for a while. Maybe he couldn't believe someone might not love Montana the way he did, that it wasn't doing for me what it did for him. "You're missing out on Montana," he said.

This sounded familiar, and I wondered if I'd evolved at all since South America. There were no rivers or horses this time to quell my longing for the ranch. So I was in no place to protest. I knew I was missing out on Montana. I went to school and walked in the same three places in the mountains that were within a ten-minute drive. I ate at the same two cheap restaurants. I didn't explore, and I didn't know any Montanans.

Smoke hung around my head, and I poured myself a beer. I don't drink beer. "There's only one place I can be," I muttered, tipping my stool back against the wall, wishing I had stuck to my usual routine.

Not long after Forest Husbands died, my Dad finally spent ten days in Mexico with his mom and sister. Before he left, he sent me a postcard for Valentine's Day—the Cascades at sunset, awash in pink. He said he hoped to return revitalized for the days of wine and roses. Dad doesn't drink wine. This was the first time he had gone anywhere without my mother since he had gone back to La Jolla twenty-eight years before. I was proud of him.

I called home the day after he got back. I talked to Mom for a little while first, but she didn't warn me. I sat on the back deck of my house in Missoula looking at the steep hills at the edge of town, wishing they would give way to the distance that surrounds my home. My dad talked so fast. A barrage of dreams and ideas.

"I need to fulfill my destiny as a human being, something more than just the ranchie. It's time to spread my wings." He talked at a clip that I could hear, but could barely understand. "There's no one at the ranch until after dark. It's cold." He skipped again, and I felt like I was being pelted. "Your mom married a surfer, and I'm still vital. I need to be with the sea and the heat."

I didn't know what to say.

"I'm going to live like you; I'll be leaving you in the dust," he said, prodding for support.

If he had given me a chance, I would have sputtered, "But Dad, I'm going the other way!"

"The plane tickets are cheap, and the endless summer is the stuff of dreams. Your mom and I went to an ATM yesterday and had a lesson in using my debit card to get money. I think I need a cell phone. She taught me how to use Subway to access fast food," he said seriously. "I am moving to the Pacific coast of Mexico for six months in the winter from now on, because I need a lot of room to be me." The ocean may be the vastest amount of room on the planet, but if there is an equivalent on land, it's the desert, where we're from. What he was really saying was he needed to get off the ranch. He was saying he didn't want to break ice; he wanted to do his art and play his guitar where the weed is cheap and the water is warm. I know that place and that life. To me, it's a lonely one. Six months would feel like a long time.

Eventually, the one-way conversation ended and left me there in the snow on the deck. I don't recall if I said anything. I suddenly felt all wrong for believing that the ranch was our place, and would be forever. He taught me how to be at the ranch. I was wrong in thinking I could teach him how to love it. I wanted to support him, but one of the biggest reasons I had invested myself in the ranch was because of him. But he didn't love it, and he was leaving—that blew my mind. I had encouraged him to leave, but suddenly I wanted to take it all back.

I wandered out to the alley and headed east toward Mount Sentinel on the edge of town. I passed the rottweiler that never barked, just charged his fence and grunted. Chyulu walked slowly beside me. I didn't get far up the mountain before I sat down in the Russian thistles. I broke one off at the ground and ripped it into tiny pieces. Without looking up, I pondered my father. I understood why he wanted to leave. I left for water too. We were at very different stages of the journey, and despite our years, I couldn't help but feel that I might be quite a bit further along. My mind wandered to my busted van on the Chilean coast and what he'd told me. "You're missing out on the people," he had said. I still was. And he was alienating himself from his people, family, and neighbors. Maybe he'd find his people—Latin, sea people, but I couldn't help but imagine him lying on the floor of a funky apartment on the Mexican coast, staring at a water-stained ceiling, looking for himself.

THE WRONG TURN

Not long after Dad's phone call, I went home for spring break. The house had come a long way since I'd left the year before. I had managed to get a roof on it during miscellaneous two-week stints at home. It was insulated and covered on the inside with beautiful tongue-and-groove pine. During this visit, my goal was to get the windows in.

I pulled up the driveway at sundown and stepped out. I couldn't see the change, but I could feel it. I had pushed hard over snowy passes to make the drive in a day. My butt and back ached, and my eyes felt strained. Chyulu lowered himself out of the car and looked quite disoriented before stretching and yawning. Dad had just finished flicking some hay to the horses and met me with a heavily clad hug.

"Gawd. You're always in an all-fired hurry to get back here, and you never want to leave." He stepped back and looked at me.

I furrowed my brow, not sure what to make of such an aggressive comment. "Yeah, it's my spot," I said.

Dad flipped his head. "Well, I just can't see why."

I didn't respond. I understood that he wanted to go, but why the hell was he belittling the ranch? It was his life's work, whether he liked it or not, and it was a good place. It represented family and work and love and determination and commitment. Why couldn't he remember that life is nothing without home and family, even when you have to leave them? He looked out into the dusk at my horses eating behind the house. The mule raised her head and turned her long, soft ears toward us.

"When are you going to break that mule?" he asked and gestured toward her with his chin.

I waited until he looked back at me, then, making eye contact with him, I said tersely, "When she's old enough."

"Seems like you should ride those horses or sell them." Dad had always said my horses could stay at the ranch until they died of old age. He'd always ridden my good gelding anyway, but since he got home from Mexico he'd stopped. His words hurt.

He had a chronic cough and his teeth looked bad, his skin leathery and his hair shaggy white. What had happened? A reunion with water should have made him more full of life, not the opposite. He was obsessed with leaving, but he knew he would have to wait until he was done farming in October. Another looming summer made him stop work and start drinking his beer and tequila with lime at three in the afternoon, when he played his guitar on the deck.

The way he flip-flopped in our phone conversations frightened me. One day he'd be hell-bent on hunting coyotes to sell their hides, and the next day they were God's creatures and taking pictures of them was more appropriate. He always said he would live out his days on the ranch, but lately he was calling it his 401(k), which left me feeling terrified and vulnerable about losing my place. When we put up the pine ceiling, he said we had to have a nail gun, and when it jammed he said nail guns were for fat people. Now he wouldn't even keep my horses.

He stood in front of me, oddly silent. I felt like if I squinted just right I could see him quaking there like the aspen leaves in October, frost-blackened, ready to fall. I didn't trust him. I had driven home to see him and work on the house, but I felt afraid to work with him. The house was our base. We'd worked together so long up there that I felt we'd developed the ability to communicate and get through anything. I didn't want to find out I was wrong.

We turned and walked awkwardly to the house, where Mom had dinner ready. She took me in her arms and tilted her chin over my shoulder. "I'm glad you're home," she said. We sat down at the table and ate. No conversation, just utensils tinkling against plates and the woodstove roaring.

The next morning, despite my fears, Dad and I loaded his new saw in the truck to cut out the holes for my windows. When I turned on the radio, he turned it off. I opened and closed the two wire gates, and we drove in silence through the rocky pasture to my house. We worked all day, marking the holes and cutting them out. I stood back while he made a cut, letting the sawdust fall all over me. I glared at my feet as my mind wandered. The fact that I was certain about where I belonged felt like such a gift. And I always felt like my dad had given me that gift, carefully handing it down. I thought I was in training for the future, to take care of him in the house that he built. But it was becoming clear that he had simply drawn me back there at an important time in my life, helped me build a home, and now he was headed for the sea. It was up to me to stay there if that's what I wanted, but he didn't seem to care either way. The generational feeling of the ranch was crumbling. Yes, I would be the next generation, but his link in the chain would go missing. He was stepping out of my dream, that I would have kids and he'd be the grandfather playing with them every day after school.

He killed the saw and set it down. We took out our earplugs and eyed the cut with a level. "I know you need to go, Dad, but what's so wrong with this place?" I said suddenly, still looking at the level.

"I can't hold the course." He took a swig of water with a hint of tequila. "I try not to overthink my course of retiring from all that has held me in its caress, my folks, my wife, the land, my horses, my memories." Putting the lid back on his battered plastic water bottle, he said, "I'm not new to the deal of memories and am livin' to mix it up in the Mex, where's I can surf and you all are welcome to visit *my* place."

I snapped another chalk line and moved to the next window with my measuring tape and level. I wondered if the sea was not only his place, but also his love. The difference between us seemed that no matter the love affair I had with rivers, home held me in a way that no other place could. Dad had clearly fallen out of love with the ranch and everything to do with it entirely. I had listened to him play his guitar the night before, out on the deck in the dark. He was singing his own lyrics and crying. I sat around the west side of the house where he couldn't see me. Slumped down on some rocks, I rested my head in my hands, tears dropping through my fingers into the dust. I knew how he felt. Water had ahold of me, too. I had to push myself to the ends of the earth before I wanted to come back to the ranch, and even then I still had to leave. But it sounded like he would never come back. And it broke my heart.

We finished work on the house and went to dinner at Mamsy and Bompa's house. Dad had been drinking and got mad about something no one understood. He pushed back his chair and stood, staggering. He yelled at somebody about something. Explosive behavior was nothing new in our family. My grandfather was known for blowing up and walking off when I was a kid. So, when Dad left us there, our plates heaped with steak and potatoes and spinach salad, we let him go. Mamsy tried to ignore the commotion and asked how people liked the food. We finished dinner. Mom and I did the dishes and served homemade apple pie with tea. Eventually we walked home.

Mom and I walked arm in arm, balancing each other while we looked up at the stars. We could see our breath in the moonlight as we made the trek without turning on the flashlight. She didn't say anything about Dad's explosion, so I didn't either. Suddenly, Chyulu stopped and gave a deep woof. Chyulu never barked. Mom and I stopped and looked out into the horse pasture ahead of us. I could see a shadow faintly moving, maybe a horse lying down. Mom couldn't see anything. Her night vision was terrible. Chyulu held by our side as we approached the fence.

"Hello," I yelled into the night and squinted my eyes to see. As we got closer I heard a retching sound. It was Dad, on his hands and knees, puking in the dirt. Light from the full moon sifted through thick cloud, and Mom rushed to him. She grabbed a shovel and started covering up his puke, maybe to protect the dog or to pretend this wasn't happening, I'm not sure. It was only March, but the ground was already dust. Dad screamed out for God to help him. He hollered that he was tired of living. He wiped his mouth on his sleeve and crawled toward the house, leaving two broad lines in the dirt where his feet trailed behind him. His head ran into the smooth wire fence and set him back. Mom shone the light on him. "Do you think you have the flu?"

"No," he said. "I have you."

Chyulu cowered at a distance. The air was still and cool. I picked up the hat I had knitted him and shook off the dust and dry manure. I stood by while he crawled. Finally I asked, "Can I help you?"

He stopped. "You don't represent help."

I did not respond. I felt empty, not mad or sad. Nothing. He crawled up the back step and groped for the doorknob. The door swung open, and he fell through onto the linoleum floor. We took his dirty clothes off so he was lying there in his little white undies. I grabbed him under the shoulders and Mom took hold of his feet and we carried him to bed. He lay there for hours, weeping and moaning.

I sat with Chyulu, our backs to the fire, as we listened to Mom run her bath. She would ease into her claw-foot bathtub every night, letting the day and the worries and the work melt off her body and sink to the steel bottom before draining away. Then I heard it, that first gasp when a person breaks down and cries. It was my mother, crying for the first time. I leaned back in my chair and listened to my parents' cries from opposite ends of the house they'd built. I wondered if they could even hear each other over themselves, and I wished they would lie together and let all those tears wash over them. I imagined the heaving coming to an end and that somehow they'd be on the other side of all of this. But instead I listened for a long time before I finally stood and walked slowly to the bathroom. I stood outside the door for a long moment, scared to actually see her cry. I felt like my rock was crumbling, but I walked in anyway. She stood bent over the counter with her face in her giant hands. Her naked body trembled; her long legs stretched down to her toes that curled and pulled together. All she wore was her little white shower cap. My body felt empty, not choked up at all. My heart didn't even race. I just stepped to her and put my arms around her shuddering body, leaning forward to rest my head on her shoulder blade.

ROCKS

After what felt like the saddest night of my life, Mom and I decided to go for a drive to collect rocks. We needed some time, just the two of us. We needed a break from Dad. I had finished the logs and roof, and it was time to put Geraldine's stove at the center of the house, where it belonged. The mantel rocks would be basalt from the Swedish Flats along Squaw Creek. Mom had been eyeing those rocks for years.

Chyulu sat in the middle of the bench seat in the old Chevy pickup, between Mom and me. The day was clear and crisp, and you could feel the sun. Sometimes the sun either gets blown off your skin or it bends and misses you, but that day was warm as we bounced out the dirt road toward the creek crossing. We didn't say anything about the night before, not yet. Instead we just bounced along quietly until she said, "These are the Swedish Flats." She knew I was endlessly fascinated by random historical tidbits. "The folks who settled here cleared this flat-top, rock-riddled ground and truly believed water would come."

I nodded and looked west over the flats while I twirled Chyulu's ear with my left hand.

"But you see how the ground falls off in every direction? Well, they had to carry water up here from the creek until they finally gave up and essentially blew away." She put two hands on the wheel to navigate a steep, rocky section of the road.

My mind had been circling around my Dad's meltdown like a pack of coyotes. But for a moment I took a break and started to wonder about my own house that I had built off the grid, and where my water would come from. Water flowed south through the ranch in a complex watershed of main streams, tributaries, rivulets, and reservoirs. It flowed naturally from the northwest corner of the land when it rained. Irrigation water in the summertime came from the main canal that marked the upper perimeter of the land. Our irrigation water was diverted down a leaky little ditch that had created its own ecosystem, at least until the pipeline went through. Frogs and fish and cattails and willows could never survive in the sage and juniper desert. The ditch flowed down through two holding ponds. We called them the upper and the lower. In the winter, the ponds were dry and didn't seem to catch any natural runoff, which made me wonder if they could have been better placed.

It felt good to let my mind wander away from the depressing times at hand. I thought about myself as a child, damming the ditch in the spring, working frantically as the first water of the season came trickling down to blow out my mud and rock obstructions. I caught frogs. The bright green ones were my favorite. And I caught the same garter snake for many years. I recognized him by the scar on his head. I would take him home for a couple of weeks and tote him around until I got tired of his stink and returned him to that narrow strip of green between the ponds.

The lower pond had a tendency to blow out on its low side when we couldn't keep our levels just right. Sometimes we turned the wheel line off to save water, but the pond couldn't hold the water, and it all went spilling out over the brim into one of the two natural drainages on the place. The other drainage was uphill and to the west. My house sat between the two. The lower drainage seemed to wash directly toward my folks' house. Luckily it swung just to the left of the house and down to the right of the chicken coop before most of it seeped into the sandy soil to the south.

I built my place higher up on our minuscule watershed than my parents had, but it had its fair share of drainage issues. The main spring creek circled my small hill to the west through deeper sandy soil. The wee tributary seemed to start from nowhere behind the house and funneled into a stream that trotted right past my northeast corner before it hit the old wagon road's hardpan ditch, where it made a ninety-degree turn and ran down to meet the main water-way. That little piece of water was solely responsible for the muddy morass around the house that had brought construction to a screeching halt at times. It was the reason we buried the gravel truck and had to build a road. You couldn't even see it. It ran under the surface.

I was planning to collect our seven inches of annual rainfall off my metal roof for domestic use. If seven inches of rain fell on my 1,200 square feet, that would be 5,236 gallons per year. The water would be used only for bathing, cooking, and drinking, because I would have a composting toilet. If it took an average of twenty gallons per day to shower and ten gallons for cooking and drinking, then that would be 10,950 gallons used per year. That meant I could collect only half of the water I would use in a year, in a best-case scenario. I reassured myself that in the summer I would use a small amount of irrigation water. Also, I put together enough hose to reach from the standpipe at my parents' well to my house, like a long umbilical cord, when I was mixing concrete for my foundation. I could use this to slowly fill the four-thousand-gallon tank I had traded for by hauling hay. I patted Chyulu with a grunt and thought, "I will not dry up and blow away."

Mom pulled to the side of the road and turned off the engine. "Here we are."

I grabbed my gloves and set out over the dryground looking for the flat rocks that Mom had seen twenty years ago when the whole neighborhood was chasing our new Brangus bull, who had escaped and busted through fences and counties for three days. She had noted that the rocks on this high piece of ground would be perfect for a woodstove mantel. It seemed crazy to me, maybe circular, to be back at these rocks. Maybe I was a little surprised they were still there.

The rocks were beautiful, with burnt orange and yellow lichen. They were dark basalt, probably deposited there 5.3 million years ago by a group of cinder cones called the

Tetherow Buttes. The lava that poured out of the buttes created prominent rimrock that capped the mesas surrounding Lower Bridge. Volcanoes were responsible for the formation of most of the rocks formed in Oregon over the past forty-five million years. It made me wonder how much a person is a product of their land. My volatile father may well have been hooked into an explosiveness that went back well beyond comprehension.

Our position at the edge of the North American crustal plate is where a small oceanic plate is being subducted from the west, creating fresh magma, which rises and erupts in the Cascade Range to the west. A long line of volcanoes catch winter snows and ease the water to us in the spring. They were the most constant presence we had amid all the human development on the eastern slope. Those steep talus slopes seemed to be the only thing that could impose a limit on second homes and golf courses.

To the east of us, Smith Rock lay at the head of Grizzly Butte. The whole formation looked like a giant sleeping dragon backed by the sunrise. The six-hundred-foot rock massif with castellated vertical cliffs constitutes a small rhyolitic volcano in the John Day Formation. The rock was indurate tuff that was generated by violent explosions resulting from the chance interaction of rising magma and shallow groundwater. The water quenched the magma and turned it to glass that was pulverized and ejected as fine ash when the water was explosively converted to steam.

Most recently, Newberry Crater to the south overflowed with black glass obsidian flows. We would find the remnants in sandy draws where Native Americans left arrowheads they had chipped out of obsidian around abandoned hunting camps. And to the north, Columbia River basalt swept in fearsome fissure eruptions as the continent overrode the Yellowstone hot spot during the Miocene epoch some fifteen million years ago. The hot spot torched its way across southern Idaho and now sits at the corner of Wyoming and Montana beneath the geysers of Yellowstone National Park, far from dead.

We collected sixty-eight oddly flat rocks in a sea of hardened lava droplets, forty-four of which nestled perfectly onto a four-foot-by-four-foot section of floor and a four-foot-by-four-foot backboard. I had no masonry experience, but I bought my mortar and grout and set to it. On Monday, Mom went back to work, and I hid out at my house while Dad thrashed around in his shop.

The bottom rocks went down easily, as I nestled them in a thick bed of mortar. The next day I slathered the backboard with mortar and pressed rocks into it. As I moved up the wall, I got a little too ambitious. Setting one too many caused five just-set rocks to peel off. I panicked and slapped them back up, bracing them with buckets and boards so they could set. After that I put up only one rock at a time.

Mom had left for work early one day, so I fixed eggs, bacon, and toast for Dad. He was quiet, his face pained like it had been for days since his meltdown, as he silently beat himself up. Eventually I couldn't stand it anymore. I was scared to know what was on his mind, but I needed to know and he needed someone to listen. "What are you thinking about?" I asked.

He didn't pause at all. "Its cold, Sarah. Winter is so heavy, and I've been a servant to this land all summer . . . forever. I watch the warm months get away while I work and work and work and nick and frick at this land, and now it's cold. And my bones are old and cold, and I am now a bird on the wing and I've got to go. I want to go to Mexico. I want to go where I can play and stay warm and surf. I want to paddle out and catch waves. I want to paint and hang out. I measure the fuck up all summer and I need a break." The diatribe went on and on as he shoveled his eggs in his mouth, his face crumpling and contracting. Every wrinkle at full depth. Every vein at full extension. He scraped the last bit of egg yolk up with the back of his fork, stuck it into his mouth, then dropped the fork on the plate. I jerked at the sound, slowly putting another small bite in my mouth. He grabbed his plate and stomped to the kitchen, flicking the faucet on full blast.

"You got to leave, Sarah. We supported you, and you ran with it. You lived extravagantly, and you saw the world. You jumped all over every opportunity you ever had. You ran rivers. You got your water; you got so much of it that you couldn't handle any more. Do you know how bad I want that? How bad I want the sea? You might be back now, but how did you feel leaving here at fifteen? I'll tell you. You couldn't wait to get the hell out of here. You hit that road and didn't look back. I missed my chance at parenting when we were both younger. You grew up in a bigger world and now you're back to parent me. That's what it feels like."

He rammed the dishes under the faucet, spraying water all over the counter and himself. Tears started to burst out of him, literally flying out of his face. I just sat there, looking blankly at him. Listening quietly. Letting him get it out, get it all out, let it go, get it out in the open so we could go forward, so we could figure this out, figure out what he needed.

"And you love this fucking hot, fucking cold desert, and that's all well and good. You're just starting. I've been here for twenty-eight years. And this is my chance. This is my chance to see the world. You'll be here for the winter and you'll love it, because that's just how you are, but come summer, you'll go. You'll have a river to run. And you know what? I'll say, have a good time. Take a break. I won't let you forget it. I won't let you forget that I let you go and I held the line here. I measured up. And because of that, you can come and go as you please. And I'll respect it, because everyone needs a break from this place."

He just kept talking, and I listened. "But I'll miss you and my dogs and my cat. I will. It will be hard for me. I get lonely, but if I wait for you and Christina, I'm gonna wait my whole life. These are my last vital years. I'm getting old. You left, and Christina went to town, and you guys get away, you have social interactions. But that's not me. I wait here in the cold for someone to come home in the dark. I'm lonely. I'm tired. I'm bored. I'm cold. It's been over ten years of that, since you left and your mom got that job, and you know what? I got over it. I got over needing you guys. I need to feel warm and vital even if that means I have to do it alone."

He was so conflicted, and of all the feelings he was having, I could understand that one the best. I had to make myself go every goddamn time, and every time I asked myself why in the hell I had to go so bad if all I wanted to do was stay, but I went and I believed I was better for it. But I didn't say anything. I didn't know what to say or what to do. He slammed the last dish in the rack and walked out. Walked right out. And as the door slammed, the wall I had built to keep myself together, to keep a straight face, a silent face, crumbled in front of me. I wept into what was left of my eggs, cold like mucus. This seemed so sudden, even if maybe I knew that it had been coming my whole life, building a little bit every day. Now he was erupting. There wasn't anything I could do to fix it. Nothing my mom could do either. She worked so they could afford to stay at the ranch. She got two weeks off a year. She couldn't go with him. She couldn't keep him happy, there or away. All she could do was watch; watch him lose his mind. Dad and I certainly couldn't go together. We couldn't both leave Mom there with the horses and dogs and cat and ice in the water troughs and snow in the driveway, all in the dark on both ends of her long workdays. I'd never felt so helpless in my life. How could he be so lonely when I spent every day with him? My mind raced around behind blurred eyes until they refocused and weren't crying anymore. The tears had dried, so I picked up the plate, set it in the sink, and walked outside without any kind of purpose or confidence. I didn't have any resolve or answers. Just confusion and helplessness, with the cold on my face and my hands, my canvas layers heavy on my body.

Two weeks later, I used the old Farmall 550 to haul the stove from my parent's garage to my house. Dad was packing up his shop, throwing things in boxes, throwing things away. He didn't have any plan, but somehow he was heading to

Mexico and it could be any day, by God. Mom helped me install the stovepipe and collect kindling. I knelt in front of the stove with my small dry pieces of kindling, some paper, and a couple of small logs, and laid a fire. I scrunched the paper and piled it in the middle, then set two small logs either side of the fluffy pile to hold it together. I leaned my kindling against the paper so it looked like the poles of a tee-pee, opened the flue and reached for my matchbox. I paused for a moment, thinking Dad would walk in. Striking a match, I lit the paper at the base of the pile and watched the flames lick up between the kindling. I closed the door and sat back on my heels. I felt like a little girl at Geraldine's house, letting my eyes go hazy on the flames. I couldn't believe my dad wasn't there with me. This whole project felt like the most immense failure. My mom put her hand on my shoulder, and I shook my head. Then stubbornly I thought to myself, every night that I sit by this stove, pulsating with heat, I'll think of my cold, dry room in Cusco and Dad's letter that brought me the heat. He would always be there with me, no matter what, and maybe there was a hint of success in that.

THE BITTER END

E ventually, we had to talk as a family about what would
happen next. After a silent dinner, Dad got up to wash
the dishes while Mom and I sat at opposite ends of the table.
I looked at her, hoping she would say something to him, but
she just sat there, stoic. I pulled threads out of the tablecloth
and balled them between my fingers. Chyulu flopped at my
feet, and I caught my reflection in the picture window. As
Dad shuffled back to the table to collect the rest of the dinner dishes, Mom finally spoke.

"What do you need?" she said without shifting her steely eyes.

Dad stopped by the edge of the table, then stepped back.
I felt like I could see the fuse, a crackling light moving up
his body. He stood there shirtless, his wiry body flushing red
with anger. His brow became a crevice, deep like cleaved
soil from a flood. He raised his hand, straightening his palm,
then brought it down like a hatchet.

"I've given you almost thirty years of my life, and that's all I can give," he said as he thrust his hand forward, claiming his path. We were a job, and he was retiring. He shot his glare at each of us, then at his own reflection in the window. "I have to get back to the ocean. Twenty-eight years of land-lock is like shackles of iron on my soul." He paused. "This life ain't gonna use me anymore. I've been under it for years. I can't live with your fear, and you can't live with mine."

Mom tilted her head to look at him, then nodded. None of it was a surprise to her. She had encouraged him to take breaks and go to the beach, but he didn't want to go without her. All those years we thought him content enough; other-wise he would have gone. But when he went to Mexico, it was like the warm ocean tore off all his old scabs. Now he was standing there raw and bleeding.

Mom and I sat back. With no other option, we needed to look at his leaving realistically. We talked logistics. How long did he want to be away? How much would it cost? Who would do his work while he was gone, and would he come back? Dad never sat down; he stood stiffly under the purlin of his house while Mom and I made a budget. Mom plugged numbers into a calculator while I made notes. We calcu-lated mileage and the cost of diesel, food, and lodging. Then we looked at the cost of the ranch. They bought the ranch together twenty-five years before for $32,100, and together they had built it into a spread worth $740,000, on paper. The previous year, they wound up $833.44 in the hole. They made $70,000 between them, and the ranch swallowed it up. In the end, we figured he could have six months and $5,000, but it would take a lot of work and budgeting.

Mom finally looked at him. Dad's face seemed frozen in distress. His feet were firmly planted on the floor, and his muscles knotted, quivering under his thin, brown skin. I felt like I could see the effects of twenty-five years on the ranch hanging on his body. He looked down at Mom, and she said, "I'll hold down the fort while you're gone if you chop the firewood before you go."

Dad turned to me and I cleared my throat and said, "I'll spend my break on the pipeline for you."

He held his lips tight and frowned. "This place has taken my body. My ass is falling out from driving tractor over these fields of gopher mounds," he cursed, as if it were the land's fault.

Mom and I looked away. Couldn't he hear what we were saying? We were letting him go. We were doing everything in our power to make it happen and then some. He was pushing us to the edge of our tolerance. He was a small, explosive man, provoking two big, fiery women. I gritted my teeth and pulled on Chyulu's ear. Chyulu opened his sleepy eye and looked at me. Dad was right when he said the ranch was austere. It was indeed lonely, and soon only women would live there. That night we committed to taking on the burden he couldn't stand.

"You love the ranch," he shouted, looking down at Mom, who didn't look back. "I worked hard to get this place to where it is today. And I did it for you." He tried to catch her eye, but she wouldn't respond. "You have a place where you're happy, and that should be good enough. Now I need to find *my* place."

I gritted my teeth as my world crumbled in front of me. Chyulu yelped as I pulled a little too hard on his ear. I could see a tremendous core in my father, and it both terrified and inspired me. He left the dishes unwashed in the sink and marched to his bedroom. I thought the door would slam, but it shut softly. Mom sat at the end of the table, her face nearly expressionless. I felt the heat of the fire on my back and let go of Chyulu's ear. I waited until Dad had gone to bed before I cried.

With a quivering voice, I told Mom, "I'll be here."

She sat down in the chair beside me and held out her left hand. "My wedding band broke the day he got back from Mexico." She pulled her hand back and looked down.

I felt blindsided, shocked by the way he was treating us, as if we'd treated him the same way. "Have we kept him here, in the dark, like a kid in the basement?" We didn't look at each other. "Is this our fault? Is there any way we could have changed the course of all of this?"

Mom didn't look up, but said in a voice laden with more sadness than anything I had ever heard, "I'm afraid of the future. Every time I think of the future, I take a wrong turn in my mind." She couldn't imagine him going and coming home happier. She saw him drunk, acting on bad judgment and getting thrown in jail. She saw him with other women. She saw herself cold and alone and bound to the ranch with horses to feed, an empty, cold, bitter dream. The place was too much work for one person if that person had a full-time job in town. "I'm just trying to survive," she said.

In a sense, Dad had spent the past twenty-eight years as a gardener. He hadn't put down his own roots; he'd put down my mom's and mine. I had flourished as if I were one of his perennial plants. I leaned back and wondered, what happens to an abandoned garden? I guessed plants either die or go native. If they belonged there, in the larger scope of things, then they'd survive—a bit smaller, adapted, fitting in where they could.

SWEAT PRAYERS

I crawled into the sweat lodge, moving clockwise, and found my place in the musty dark. The Native American men came in last. Under the dome's skeleton, made from willows and covered in wool blankets, the stones in the center were red-hot and considered the grandmothers and grandfathers of the Northern Cheyenne. The leader of the ceremony sprinkled cedar chips on the rocks and dropped the flap. I was back in Montana for school. Time had rolled by like a giant stone wheel—loud and rough, all of us barely making it through another summer before Dad would be allowed to go. I had taken a break from graduate school to run the Yellowstone River in eastern Montana and had driven south for a visit to the Northern Cheyenne reservation.

The first water hit the rocks with a hiss. Hot vapors hit the ceiling and curled toward our bodies. The red of the rocks blinked out one by one as more water hit the pile.

Complete, thick darkness. I sang songs I didn't know, louder and louder as it got hotter and hotter. And through the song, I prayed, maybe for the first time in my life.

I prayed for my dad. I prayed that his journey would be safe and full and that the majority of his days would be peaceful, with the sea and art and hot days with big shade. And that the days that would inevitably be hard would pass quickly with firm resolve. That in the face of fear and loneliness he wouldn't miss the fullness of those feelings. That he would cry to let go and then grasp reality with his heart. I prayed that he would find what could make him whole again after so many years of longing. I prayed that the ocean would break and the saltwater would cleanse him. I prayed that it would eventually send him home.

I prayed for myself, too. I prayed for forgiveness and strength. Before, I had hoped that Mexico wouldn't be what he was looking for, because I was afraid of the ranch without him. I was afraid of taking his place, alone on the desert. So I prayed for strength in the journey that would take me to the end of the driveway and no farther. And when he disappeared around the bend in the road, the strength to walk home . . . to "walk the walk," as Dad would say. To till the field and fix fence and keep the fire going and bring in the wood and clean the dishes at lunchtime and flick the feed, and when I have to go, to go bravely, and then to return to build my life on the ranch, waiting patiently for when we get to be together again. To hang on, but to do so in the most loving, eternally patient way, just as he did through all my leaving.

The flap on the sweat lodge went up, and the steam billowed out into the clear dark. The orange light of the fire hit my face and the fire chief stepped out. Steam spun up his dark, thick body as he grabbed a pitchfork and started extracting new rocks from the fire. He carried them carefully to the center of the lodge and added them to the pile of rocks. Our faces glistened. My whole body was wet. I could feel toxins coming to the surface and dripping away.

The fire chief ducked back in, and the flap dropped. Again the red rocks blinked out with the water and rose into steam. And I sang. I sang, and I began my prayers again. I sent them to Dad, and I sent them south, where they'd be waiting when he arrived. The prayers know the way to the perfect spot. Where the months will ease by and through him.

The salt from my skin dripped into my eyes, which I opened wide to the darkness. Song flowed out of me unconsciously. The steam was hot in my nose and lungs. I opened my hands, palms up, and set them beside me, then dropped my head and closed my eyes. I listened for the other voices. I listened to the words of the Northern Cheyenne.

The last song died down to a low hum and the light tap of two sticks. Then it was silent, for a long moment. When the flap went up and the fire chief stepped out, we moved out clockwise and stood in the clear, cold night. My head felt light. I moved to the bonfire and watched the steam lick up my stomach. Sitting down in the dust, I pulled a piece of paper and a pen out of my bag and scribbled a letter to my father.

Dear Daddy,
The bumper of your truck is pointed straight south.
Or maybe west. Maybe you're looking at perfect,
warm little barrels and an empty beach. You have

arrived. To the place of your healing. To a place you can be free. To let go of the confines of your flesh. A place you are not fighting. You can bob in the salt-water and eat fish and watch the sun slip by.

I'm going to miss you so much. But when I do, I'll drink a beer with some lime and get up in the night to look at the stars. I'll lie in front of the fire after lunch and play Johnny Cash. I'll braid some horse-hair and water down my drinks. But most of all, I'll run the dogs, keep them passing over this ground where you want to end up. Where someday

I've promised to spread your ashes. I'll keep the fire going. I'll ride the geldings and feed the chickens. I'll keep the hose thawed, and I'll try to make some new gates. I'll wait and watch the driveway.
Vaya con dios, das vi danya, as Bompa would have said. You're a good man, and you will be missed.

Your Sarahlee

THE RIGHT TURN

I returned in November to see Dad off. I had hoped to support my mother through the transition, but it turned out that Dad was the one who needed support. He hadn't packed. He hadn't bought a tank of gas at a gas station since you could stick your credit card in the pump. And he was about to leave for six months in Mexico. I did what I knew how to do. I packed for him. I had been leaving my whole life, and for the first time I was the one to stay. I filled up his tires with air, checked the oil in the truck, and washed his windshield, the same things he had done for me on the morning of every one of my departures. I kept busy; I didn't want to talk. I was on the edge of tears and didn't want to cross over.

The sunrise on the day he left made everything drip with pink light. I walked out to his rig and climbed up between the truck and horse trailer into the camper. I left some pictures and my letter under his pillow and a jar of soil, juniper, and sage in his cupboard. When I opened his trailer to add a pair of jeans to the Tupperware bin of clothes that I had packed for him, I smiled as I scanned over the surfboards, canoe, sewing machine, chain saw, bicycle, saddle, cases of beer, art supplies, guitar, and lawn chair. The load didn't look much different from the trash I loaded in the trailer to take to the dump.

Mom and I talked about the strange new path ahead of us while Dad tried to find things in his shop for me to pack. We were all embarking on a new chapter of our lives. I tried to remember the Tambopata and the way I was able to embrace the unknown. And that by embracing it, I made it through to the other side—alive. Mom said she was joyful and that she admired Dad for changing his life, though we knew no one would understand. She had always told me, when I brought my garter snakes home in the spring, that if I loved something I had to set it free. When she spoke she sounded like deep, dark, calm water.

The day Dad left was warm and still, clear and bright. Perfect. Before I knew it, he was pulling out the driveway. I hoped he would wonder why he was leaving in this way; he took everything he owned and refused to mention his return. He turned right out of the driveway and headed south. He was about to unwind the circles he'd driven around the hay fields for thirty years and stretch them down the highway.

He honked, and I thought about what he must be feeling. I had pulled out of the driveway a hundred times, but I always knew I would return. I had put a Johnny Cash CD in his stereo, and I imagined him turning the volume up as tears filled his eyes. The road ahead would get blurry, and he'd try not to look in the rearview mirror, but by the time he'd driven the ten miles to Terrebonne, he'd be settling into his bench seat for the long haul.

He left a wake. It took me days to adjust to being at the ranch alone. I thought I knew how to care for the place. I got in the habit of feeding the horses, dogs, chickens, and cat twice a day; I moved hay around and broke ice. Mom walked out with me one day to break ice and said, "I broke ice and carried water all day for three weeks once from only one standpipe, while the temps stayed below zero." I'd heard the story before, but she kept telling it anyway. "I wasn't so sure about central Oregon, but I'm glad I didn't give up." It was what she said next that made me think. "And now you're here, brave girl. After all your travels, you've come home to break ice." She smiled and nudged my shoulder, and I smiled a little bit for the first time in a while.

It was when I tried to start disking the field for next year's seeding that I got lost. After all those years, I didn't know how to service and run the big tractor on my own. I'd driven it, but I'd never started the thing. Slumping down against its great big tire, I felt small and out of place. The big tractor was parked right near the road, and just as I was about to cry, Glen Cooper pulled up the driveway because he saw my truck.

"Hello, Sarah," he said. "Looks like you're about to disk your dad's field."

"Not really, Glen. I don't know how."

"Oh, come on, girl, it's easy. You've been here your whole life."

My head dropped. "I know, Glen, that's why I feel like such a piece of shit."

He wasn't the most compassionate man, so I was surprised when he said, "Well, I'll help you get started and
hooked up. You'll know what to do from there."

I got right up without an ounce of mope in my step and
stood with him by the tractor while he pointed out where
to check all the fluids. Then we climbed on board and he
showed me how to use all the levers and buttons, how to
steer a four-wheel-drive tractor, which bends oddly in the
middle. We fired it up and backed up to the disk, then headed
to the field. He told me about methods of disking, how to pay
attention to my engine, how to keep an eye on the piece of
equipment behind me. He told me everything I needed to
know, and I wondered how come my dad hadn't taught me
any of that over the course of my life. I wondered if it was
just that I hadn't cared to learn, or that he hadn't cared to
teach me. Before Glen eased down off the tractor, leaving me
there on my own, he asked me to help him on the pipeline
the next day. I told him I would be happy to.

It takes many passes with the disk to break up the sod. I put
in my earplugs and tried to get a feel for the ground, what it felt
like to wind all those miles into a circle like a tight ball of yarn.
And I thought about how Dad and I seemed to run with our
backs to each other. I watched people drive by and wondered
where they were going. I also wondered how long I would be in
that place until I, too, would feel the urge to run another river. It
occurred to me that maybe a person with an addiction to water
should not live in the high desert. Water is always a problem in
the desert: either there's too much of it or not enough.

The next day, Glen and I lay in a pile of plastic shavings
from the pipe we were welding for the pipeline, our hats

pulled down over our eyes to keep the blowing dirt out. We waited the forty minutes for another plastic weld to cool. I offered him a carrot and some hummus. He declined, but I handed him one anyway. Silly hippie food, he was thinking. He bit it off and chewed, blankly.

"What do you think?" I asked.

"It's okay," he said. "I try not to eat things I don't know."

"It's good to take adventure bites, Glen."

When the timer went off, I fired up the dozer, pulled my hat over my eyes and nose to keep the ash and fumes out, then plugged my ears. When I sat down in the seat, all I could see was my canvas jacket front speckled with rain-drops, a pink silk scarf, and a long brown braid blown south over my left shoulder. I slowly eased the machine forward, directed by Glen, and pulled the pipe through the machine until it was in line for the next weld. When I walked back to the welder to help him position the next piece of pipe, I leaned patiently against the heater plate for him to give me my next instructions. I stood there wondering if Glen had me in mind when he worked on the pipeline all win-ter long. I wondered if he thought I'd make a good farmer, and whether I deserved the water to make a go of it. After all, I was the next generation, and the only real one in the whole valley. It felt good to spend the day with him, talking about hauling his family up from California with no more than $500 to his name. I listened to stories about his tours in Europe as a military diesel mechanic and his old girlfriend that he'd recently been reunited with after parting ways in high school. I didn't think a whole lot about Dad when I was with Glen, and I appreciated that.

A while after Dad left, Mom and I cleaned out his shop. She told me about a study she'd heard on National Public Radio. Someone was testing the effects of marijuana on spiders. They took spiders that made perfect, orderly webs and gave them weed. The stoned spiders made discombobulated webs. They were clearly confused. As we worked through his things, we tried to rebuild his web. Dad had spent a good portion of the past thirty years riffling through his things, often giving up the search and asking Mom to pick up a new one of whatever he was looking for. We found all kinds of tools and supplies that had never been used, covered in dust. Dad had grown more and more chaotic over the years. Less efficient and more lost. I wondered if he could get hold of his mind if he quit smoking at that point, or if it was too late. It didn't really matter. He would never quit. But, after he left, I went out to his hiding spot and checked to be sure all the weed was gone. It had no business being there anymore.

One day, I went down to the end of the driveway to get the mail and look to the south. I patted Chyulu's head and let tears drip off my jaw. It had been a couple of weeks at least, and I still hadn't gotten past the sharp pain of missing him. The last thing he said to me was to find humor. He held me tight and lifted his chin over my shoulder. My arms overlapped behind him. "Laugh in the face of shit," he said.

I stood there for a long time in the stillness, looking at the road. I heard the scream of a red-tailed hawk, and my horse sneezed in the distance. Eventually I turned and walked all the way up to my house. I passed all the tractors and gas tanks, my grandparents' house and my parents' house, and then the gates we made Mom for Mother's Day. I looked into

Dad's empty shop and ducked through the smooth wire fence. When I got to my house, I climbed up on the roof to take a measurement for a stovepipe brace. The house was nearly finished, and finally, I wasn't concerned with time anymore. I sat up there and looked out over the tops of the trees with this sense that my life felt so much like a river, the way it changed and flowed into the unknown. I admired the mountains and the home beneath me. I thought about reading *Walden* in the jungle and all that had happened since then. I said to myself, "I built a whole house once just so I could spend time with my Dad," and smiled.

When I climbed down, I walked inside and stood in the sunlight that streamed across the floor to the north wall. I remembered back to the hot months when no light came in at midday and the house was cool. I knew that little spot of ground, and I belonged there. With the help of my father, I had managed to build something absolutely perfect for it. I loved that place in all its glory of mud and blowing dust, even if I was left there alone. Everything about it—the heat and cold and wind, the chapped lips, cracked fingers, and eyes full of grit—I loved.